A Family Money-

Successful Borrowing and Coping with Debt

A Family Money-Go-Round Special

Successful Borrowing and Coping with Debt

Paul Delderfield

Series Editor
Richard Northedge

Telegraph Publications

Published by Telegraph Publications
135 Fleet Street, London EC4P 4BL

Typeset by Michael Weintroub Graphics Ltd
Printed and bound in Great Britain

British Library Cataloguing in Publication Data
Delderfield, Paul
Successful borrowing and coping with debt. — (A Family money-go-round special).
1. Consumer credit — Great Britain
2. Debtor and creditor — Great Britain
I. Title II. Series
332.024'02 HG3756.G7

ISBN 0-86367-110-1

Acknowledgements

The author gratefully acknowledges the kind assistance and information given by the following organisations and individuals in the preparation of this work.

Abbey National Building Society.
Barclays Bank PLC.
Her Majesty's Stationery Office.
National Consumer Council.
National Association of Citizen's Advice Bureaux.
Building Societies Association.
Finance Houses Association.
John McQueen – Secretary, Association of Bankrupts.
Michael Sheldon-Allen for interpreting the Insolvency Act 1986.
Diane Pengelly, Marlene Garsia, Alan Wakeford and all at Telegraph Publications.
Carole Cochrane, Con M Caffee, Anne Taylor-Smith, John McLaren, Mick Kamintzi, my family, and all who believed in me, particularly Helen, my wife.

Contents

Introduction to the series

The advice to be neither borrower nor lender is impossible and unprofitable in today's world. The banks, building societies and the government itself are all eager to solicit savings from the individual – and often at attractive interest rates which are higher than the rate of price inflation. Many people are pleased that their capital is kept so safely by such institutions and that the return provides a useful contribution to their income. But it can also be profitable to pay interest *to* the banks or building societies. Most people would be unable to afford their first home without borrowing substantially more than the capital which they have actually saved themselves; store-credit allows you to buy items for the home which can be used immediately but paid for over time. Even the most prudent of us can quite sensibly become debtors therefore, even before we start using 'free credit' delaying paying our telephone or power bills until we have received next month's pay.

The problem comes when we cannot cope with all that debt. Such a situation may be because we have taken on commitments beyond our income – or because the income is no longer sufficient to meet those previously sensible commitments. It might once have seemed reckless to reach such a position, but today when high-street shops are screaming out to sell us goods on their expensive credit terms, and when unemployment or divorce can suddenly and dramatically reduce income, debt problems can face almost anyone.

It is for that reason that a book like this is necessary nowadays. Whether it is your own problem, or that of colleague or relative, this book should be able to explain how the debt crisis can be overcome. Simply knowing what exactly the consequences of the problem are and how easy it is to reduce them can remove a considerable worry for people who are being inundated with 'final reminders', red-printed letters, threats of legal action or possibly worse.

This book explains how some creditors can be expected to be more sympathetic than others; it points out that some debt is more expensive than other borrowing – and some more essential. It is likely that the debtor has assets, but does not have the cashflow to meet bills; selling those assets may occasionally be the answer but not always. It may be worth trading down from an over-large house, but it is necessary to retain some sort of home; it may also be worthwhile maintaining premiums on a life assurance policy even when you are in debt, rather than to lose its built-up value because of some temporary problem.

The Money-go-Round series of books contains many titles giving advice on investing or homebuying, but we realise that there is another side to the coin. There is already a book in this series aimed at helping couples cope with divorce or separation and the financial problems which can ensue: this book tackles another – though sometimes related – series of financial difficulties.

The Money-go-Round pages of The Daily Telegraph on Wednesday and Saturday of each week look at many of the topics covered in these books and report the day-to-day changes caused by interest rate moves, amendments in lenders' practices or changes in the law. These pages provide the most comprehensive personal finance coverage in any national newspaper, but it requires books such as these to provide detail or to collate practical information into one readily available source. It is not the intention of the books to teach readers to become experts – merely to help people to solve particular problems when they arise, or even to reassure them that they have no serious problem at all. The sound advice contained in this book – whether read from cover to cover, or simply dipped into to answer specific needs – makes it a worthy extension to the range of Money-go-Round books.

Richard Northedge
Deputy City Editor
The Daily Telegraph

Introduction

Britain is a 'debtor society' – in other words we spend more than we earn, and are encouraged to do so by the government, financial institutions and retailers, all eager to see consumer demand and thriving competition.

For most people, during the good times, debt (or credit, which is the vogue term) presents few, if any, problems. As long as we have our health and a regular income, it is possible, and can even be desirable, to live on the 'never never'. Few people, after all, can afford to buy their own homes, furniture and other essentials (not to mention the more luxurious items) with cash.

When things go wrong, however, debt is neither fun nor desirable, and can easily become a curse. Apart from the original reasons for the debt – perhaps unemployment, divorce or a sudden unexpected call on funds which are painful enough in themselves, the added financial pressures can easily lead to depression, ill-health and sometimes a complete breakdown of the debtor and his family.

Sadly, we equate our ability to repay debts with honesty and self esteem. When we cannot meet these debts, no matter what the reason, these values are called into question both personally and socially.

This book attempts to demystify the world of debt by giving the reader two insights. First, into the national problem, to provide a full perspective, and second, into private individual debt. The thrust of the work is positive, for that is what you have got to be if you are going to overcome your problem. And remember, there are always solutions to debt, even if they appear to be unpleasant and extreme. Any solution is better than jeopardising one's health or livelihood.

Most creditors are not as hard-nosed as popular myth would have us believe, and most are ready and willing to assist debtors. In fact, any creditor organisation which takes a hard line with debtors should think again. It is in their ultimate interest to help the debtors who are, after all, potential customers. They should take on greater responsibility for encouraging so many people to borrow in the first place. But the debtor must also come forward as soon as the debt problem arises. It is at this early stage that mutually acceptable solutions can most often be found.

Debt problems today are virtually unavoidable and the first point that you should understand is that you are not alone. Since 86% of adults in this country now owe money to someone else, whether it be to a building society, bank, finance house or credit card company, it is hardly surprising that each year thousands of people get into financial trouble. But while media coverage of this problem has grown still no one has tackled the problem of what people should do to avoid becoming bankrupt, or what they should do when faced with a court appearance. Look in any bookshop and you will find any number of volumes dealing with personal finance, taxation, investments and stocks and shares, telling you how to make money and keep it, but precious little on how to stop it seeping away like sand through your fingers, particularly when misfortune strikes.

The aim of this book is therefore, to inform, to counsel and to dispel any illusion about what may or may not happen as a result of being in debt. Most importantly, no moral judgements are passed on those whose debt has run out of control.

I have made no attempt to deal with the special problems surrounding divorce, single-parenthood or unemployment since there are many excellent books dealing specifically with these subjects. However, if there is a debt problem because of these circumstances, then this book will certainly point you in the right direction.

Paul E Delderfield
April 1987

Chapter One

Do you have a problem?

For many, there seems to be something final and everlasting about debt. Indeed, the very nature of borrowing implies a long-term commitment; no sooner is one agreement finalised than another is taken on, perhaps for home improvements, a boat or new car. There always seems to be something pushing you into debt and, most of the time, this is a workable, even desirable arrangement. After all, there is nothing wrong with being in debt, which is how a financial 'track record' is established – it is determined by your ability to repay commitments consistently over a given period.

Debt, though by no means a perfect state of affairs, can be an acceptable way of spreading resources to buy goods which you could not normally hope to buy in the near future. But debt does become a problem when you are unable, for whatever reason, to repay the agreed sums, at the agreed time and to the agreed party.

In 1974, the Consumer Credit Act with its subsequent amendments lifted restrictions on the giving and taking of credit. Since then the probability that people will, at some time, become unable to repay their debts has become much greater as more and more easy money has been made available. How many people now do not have at least some of the following: a mortgage, a bank loan, an overdraft, credit card(s), in-store card(s), a hire-purchase agreement, cash-flow or budget account, charge card and a loan outstanding to Auntie Flo? The more such commitments people have, the more life becomes a precarious financial juggling act where nothing they earn belongs to them. Wages immediately vanish to repay debts which could last up to 20 or 30 years.

The British are constantly being told by political and industrial gurus that they pay themselves too much, but there is little evidence to support this claim. Indeed, the British wage is small change compared with some European and Scandinavian countries, while the cost of living in the UK is comparatively high. The problem, in part, seems to be the 'affordability' of debt by people on all income levels. For example, a managing director earning £50,000 a year may have little more cash to spend than someone earning considerably less, because almost his entire income may be commited to repaying debts. Others, however, right at the bottom of the income scale, make ends meet and afford holidays and treats without becoming embroiled in debt and all its associated hazards.

Most of us have been tempted by the glowing advertisements of imagined freedom that a credit card or personal loan can bring. We can become so excited at acquiring the goods and services offered that, in many cases, the early warning signs of a problem can pass unnoticed, or even be ignored. Letters start to trickle in, slowly at first, gently but firmly making you realise that you have probably overcommited yourself. If you ignore these warning signals or postpone action until you feel that you can face your creditors, then the letters will become a flood, backed by legal threats. Do nothing at that stage and you could lose your home and everything you have worked for.

In 1983 there were over two million cases of default processed through the county courts. In around one million cases bailiffs were actually despatched to people's homes, either to evict them or to recover goods to be sold in settlement of debts. There are many ways in which some, if not most, of these unhappy circumstances could have been avoided if the debtors had known what to do when faced with the loss of home and possessions. Sadly, most did not know; neither did they know where they could go for help. After all, it is never stated on the back of a financial agreement, in clear and simple terms, precisely what could happen if you cannot pay.

Personal debt centres on a curious paradox: despite the unprecedented ease with which most of us can acquire funds for almost any (legal) purpose, the official attitude towards 'bad' debtors has hardly softened. As long as you keep your head above water – no matter how difficult it is – the lending institutions will pat you on the back and keep tempting you back for more. But default once and it is a very different story. Bad debtors are formally outcast by lending bodies and courts alike.

The debt collecting machine in this country is ruthless. Once you are in its sights, it is horribly difficult to escape. At this point many people panic and borrow more. They agree to loans at crippling rates of interest in a desperate bid to consolidate their finances. Unhappily, many of these cases end up in the county or bankruptcy courts. Faced with the possibility of financial ruin, the emotional pressure of these last ditch arrangements can all too often be the final straw, leading to the loss of home, status, and even divorce.

Fortunately, however, there are ways of solving such problems before they reach this complex and highly stressful stage.

Realism is the key

The only effective way to deal with debt is to tackle the problem head on. Many people, however, are so reluctant to acknowledge that the problem even exists that they will do almost anything rather than admit to it. But until they can stand up, like someone with a severe drinking problem at an Alcoholics Anonymous meeting to declare, 'I'm Fred and I'm a drunk', they have little hope of resolving the difficulties. Psychologically, debt must be confronted in the same way. It does not matter where or how you admit your difficulties, so long as you do. That must be the starting point, an open acknowledgment of the problem devoid of self-pity, blame or criticism. From now on you must be positive and constructive if you are going to overcome your difficulties. The sooner you are realistic in all your calculations and in the way you approach your creditors, and the sooner you draw up your plans and stick to them, the sooner you will be able to tear up all those completed agreements.

There are three ways of bringing your debts under control:

1. Increase your income.
2. Reduce your outgoings.
3. A combination of both.

Each of these has merits and disadvantages. Are you already working too hard to take on more, or have you reduced your outlay to the point that any further reduction might leave you or your dependants without sufficient food? Neither extreme is recommended. There is a middle ground which can be reached by skilful negotiation with creditors, employers, bank managers, and so on. That is the course which we will be seeking to identify and follow. Be realistic, patient and positive and success will be yours, even if, as we shall see later, bankruptcy is the only solution. Although that ordeal is certainly not a desirable solution, for some it is the only sensible way out.

Throughout this book you will find practical answers to different kinds of debt, all based on real-life situations. But each answer assumes that you acknowledge and accept responsibility for your problem, no matter what your circumstances and however much difficulty you may be experiencing with creditors. It is all too easy to blame them for your plight and end up doing nothing to help yourself even if they show a thoroughly heartless and ruthless approach to your problems. If you do encounter sympathy along the way, treat it as a bonus; it should help keep your faith in the human race intact!

If you are going to deal successfully with your debts it is essential to adopt a businesslike approach. A positive and realistic attitude should be tempered with your businesslike attitude. If you can harness these elements you will find that the stress and emotional drain on your energy will gradually diminish.

The ease of running up debts

A recent newspaper article described the plight of an unmarried woman in her mid-20s, badly in debt. She lived at home with her parents and worked as a typist earning around £130 a week gross.

She had amassed debts of £13,000 by using the 21 credit cards she had accumulated since starting work. Following her regular plastic spending sprees in the major high-street stores the day came when she could no longer meet her debts. By now, fortunately, she had exhausted the credit available from the cards and the matter came to a head. She panicked, understandably, but found that she could not tell anyone about her problem. She was too frightened to go to her bank manager in case she was offered another loan to pay off the credit card debts. Admittedly, this would have been preferable to paying each credit card company, for the saving in interest alone would have been substantial. She could not tell her parents either, since they had never been in any kind of debt and would have been unable to help financially or emotionally. Finally, in a state of suicidal depression, she contacted the Samaritans. They put her in touch with a counsellor at the local Money Advice Centre who was able to negotiate on her behalf with each of the 21 creditors. More than half of them simply wrote off the debt, fearing bad publicity, while the remainder agreed to terms which enabled her to live reasonably comfortably while still paying off her debts.

This woman was lucky that the Samaritans had put her in touch with the right people, but she was wrong to have let her financial worries depress her to the point of despair. Although it is understandable that some people should feel driven by such circumstances to suicide, it is not an option worth thinking about even for a second. There are practical answers to debt problems, but they depend on your being strong and healthy, and willing to face your problem – no matter what. No amount of worry or stress will aid your recovery, so do what you can now to put it behind you.

Chapter Two

Who gets into debt and why?

There are no national or centralised statistics revealing the extent of the debt problem, or which kinds of people typically experience difficulties in meeting financial obligations. The only information which is available is compiled largely by The Building Societies Association, Finance Houses Association and advisory agencies, such as The National Association of Citizen's Advice Bureaux and National Consumer Council. Although working on different sides of the fence, all these organisations agree about one fundamental issue: debt, particularly since 1979, has increased dramatically.

Research indicates that people on low income or receiving state benefits, or in households which experience a sudden, often unexpected drop in income, are particularly vulnerable to debt problems. The causes of the reduction in income are varied, but all can have the same unfortunate impact. Paradoxically, people within this general grouping are *not* likely to make use of credit on a wide scale and when they do ask for credit, it is often used just to make ends meet, accounting for literally every penny. If, however, they need to borrow to buy something, then credit usually takes the form of a hire purchase agreement, which is paid back fully before another is taken out.

Single parents are particularly prone to debt problems. Often restricted in the number of hours they are able to work, they may have to rely heavily on state assistance for the bulk of their income, so making it difficult to repay any loan taken out before pregnancy. In such instances it may be necessary to lengthen the repayment period.

An equally vulnerable group are young couples in the 25-40 age group, in the middle and even higher income categories. Their vulnerability may stem not only from the expectations placed upon them by other people, but also from the high expectations they have for themselves. The drain on their income through setting up home, buying furniture, cars and rearing children, can be overwhelming. If their expectations of long-term employment and security of income are not met, this can lead quickly to a reversal of fortunes. Having relied heavily on credit cards, bank loans, overdrafts and financing of all sorts in the earlier years – often to help them on to the first rung of the property ladder – can mean that what had once been a manageable loan can suddenly turn into a severe, seemingly impossible debt.

Debt: its extent and relationship to disposable income

Since 1979 personal debt as a proportion of disposable income has climbed by 60%, and is expected to reach 72% by the end of 1987. Debt as a whole consumed income by 82% in 1985, whereas the figure for 1979 stood at around 51%. It is estimated that the debt/income ratio will increase to 93% during 1987, and from this it is clear how much pressure is exerted on us to go into debt simply to keep pace with today's lifestyle.

Hire purchase and retail credit, extended and outstanding

During the period 1974-1983 the factor of extended credit rose by more than four, while the factor of outstanding credit climbed by well over five. In 1974, £2,517 million was advanced, and £2,330 million was outstanding at the year-end. In 1983, £10,524 million was extended but £12,221 million remained outstanding at the end of the year. The figures for the first half of 1986 show a spectacular increase. Credit advances at £17,700 million against £27,000 million outstanding! But what does all this mean in human terms, how does it affect the relatively small, but significant, number of people no longer able to maintain their commitments?

Repossession of homes

Repossession of homes has, tragically, spiralled upwards since 1974. There was a marked decrease in the late '70s, but the trend from 1979 has been ever upwards. In 1974, 2,860 homes were repossessed. By 1983 that figure had risen to 7,400, and in 1985 16,700 householders either voluntarily or otherwise surrendered their homes. The number of repossessions for the first half of 1986 alone was 10,630, indicating that at that rate of increase approximately 21,000 householders would be homeless by the end of the year.

Loss of the home is often the outcome of a long, hard battle for financial survival for thousands of people. The battle usually begins with the non-payment of a household bill. Gradually, if the process is not spotted early enough, funds destined to pay the mortgage are syphoned off to pay these bills because the need seems to be more pressing at the time. Consequently arrears build up and, inevitably, the mortgagee will exercise his right to the security of the property. The scale of mortgage arrears and the potential effects on homelessness are enormous.

Building society arrears 1979-84

In 1979, 8,420 building society loans were between 6 and 12 months in arrears. This number rocketed to 29,290 in 1984, and by 1985 some 100,000 householders were three months behind with building society payments. This does not include local authority mortgage loans, which occupy an increasingly significant sector of the mortgage market. In 1983 about 1½%-2% of all local authority mortgage loans were six months in arrears, accounting for about 13,000 householders.

Other facts and figures

In 1984 more than one million council tenants were behind with the rent. One million gas consumers and more than one-and-a-half million electricity customers had difficulties with bills in the year to June 1985.

Each year more than one-and-a-half million court actions or 'money plaints' are filed in the county courts – over two million in 1984 – while around one million warrants are issued for recovery of goods each year. This figure, too, is on the increase.

There is also the comparatively small community of debtors whom society either ignores or shuns, and for whom life, in most cases, exists on the margins of the state and community. These are the bankrupts. Contrary to popular myth, the great majority of bankrupts are ordinary people. Often after an excrutiating battle with the debt factors discussed above, they are either bankrupted by impatient creditors or seek the option themselves as the only means of respite from overwhelming odds. Bankruptcies usually occur among the self-employed and span the entire spectrum of occupations, from solicitors and accountants to builders and butchers. Up to 10,000 personal bankruptcy petitions are filed each year, most of which are instigated by creditors.

There is, however, a new breed of bankrupt emerging in today's financial climate – the private individual, neither self-employed nor director of a limited company. Now employees, and even the unemployed, are becoming exposed to the possibility of bankruptcy as debt consumes ever larger proportions of income.

It might seem that a major proportion of debtors or the bankrupt are somehow incompetent, reckless and, occasionally, fraudulent. It has even been a long-cherished myth that the reckless poor squander their undeserved state benefits on videos, new cars and other paraphernalia, but this is far from accurate. Mismanagement accounts for only a tiny proportion of all cases, a fact which all parties, creditors and advice agencies, are at pains to point out. Similarly, fraud accounts for only a fraction of bad debt. By far the greatest number of debtors find themselves in that predicament involuntarily; the problem is not that they do not want to wipe out their debts, but that they simply cannot do so. These people would welcome the opportunity to repay their commitments, given the good will of creditors, if the right kind of help was available. The National Association of Citizen's Advice Bureaux's figures for 1985 seem to bear this out. Around 2,342,000 enquiries relating to financial difficulties and Social Security benefits were dealt with during that year, representing 37% of all enquiries handled by the Association.

Debt and state benefits

Any financial difficulties a family may have been experiencing are immediately compounded when a breadwinner loses his job. The levels of state benefit to which households must then adjust almost guarantee financial hardship. Any household with hire-purchase agreements or credit card bills prior to unemployment would have no means whatever of meeting those commitments – unless any savings were available, and £3,000 is the current maximum allowable by law. The problem here is due, in part, to the way in which unemployment and supplementary benefit payments are calculated. It may be fair to say that help with housing costs is proportionally generous, for a claimant is normally entitled to the full amount of mortgage interest (though no capital assistance) and/or help with rent and rates. However, new Supplementary Benefit regulations introduced in November 1986 stipulate that where an unemployed claimant is a mortgage payer, he will receive only 50% payment for mortgage interest during the first four months of unemployment. Thereafter, 100% of the mortgage interest is allowed. The level of benefit provided for food, fuel bills, clothing and day-to-day expenses, however, is not apportioned in this way. It is a flat-rate payment calculated according to whether you are married, single, disabled, a single parent or have some other qualifying status.

There is clear evidence that benefit intended for housing costs is often channelled into other, more pressing areas, by claimants unable to feed their families with the statutory personal allowance. Nevertheless, it is surprising that between 1979 and 1986, when unemployment rose by over two million, the number of building society repossessions has not reflected this trend. Mortgage arrears, however, did double during this period, adding weight to the suggestion that supplementary benefits are generally insufficient to meet recipients' needs.

Fuel debt

Inability to pay fuel bills does not count as part of the overall debt statistics. The penalty for non-payment is usually disconnection, and while the fuel boards do operate codes of practice for those in financial hardship, there are still too many people who have been deprived of gas or electricity, and sometimes both.

In the 12 months to June 1985 around 32,680 domestic gas consumers and 93,940 electricity customers had their supplies cut off through non-payment of bills. In previous years the number of disconnnections was, in fact, much greater, but the fuel boards have since revised their Voluntary Codes of Practice to make payment plans available to customers with financial problems. The electricity boards have even reversed their former policy of restricting the issue of pre-payment meters. The number of pre-payment meters installed has more than doubled to around 49,000 a quarter since 1980, and now exceeds the number of cash meters being removed. It seems clear that the majority of pre-payment meters are installed instead of disconnecting customers, as the meters are calibrated to collect the arrears along with current consumption.

Another payment system evolved by the fuel boards and the DHSS is the 'fuel direct' scheme. This means that anyone claiming supplementary benefit can have part of their money deducted at source by the DHSS and paid over to the relevant fuel authority. In 1984 there were about 140,000 fuel direct cases, an increase of some 90,000 since 1980. The scheme, however, is not considered to be a success. This is partly due to the fuel boards allowing debts to build to an unrealistic level before offering the scheme as an option to customers. By this time the debt may be several hundred pounds and the amount of benefit deducted from claimants (this figure is calculated by the fuel boards without reference to claimant's other circumstances) could leave them in very serious financial hardship.

The advice agencies are calling for legislation to require fuel boards to be granted court orders before disconnections can take place. In areas where they do seek court orders, however, these are granted all too readily – the pressure of work on the courts is such that there is rarely time to investigate individual circumstances.

The first two chapters of this book have attempted a full perspective of the current scale of debt in Britain. You may not fall into the categories mentioned so far, but if you have debt problems you might draw some cold comfort from the fact that you are not alone. You are sharing a problem with millions of others. So far we have taken an impersonal look at the problem from available statistics and research. There are many millions of people, however, with an 'unofficial' problem; that is to say, they have not yet defaulted on an agreement, or are not being threatened with disconnection for non-payment of a fuel account. But, if things continue as they are, this may very well happen. This could be your situation. Or it could be worse – you may be in danger of losing your home.

Getting into debt is easy, as you may have discovered. Getting out of it is another matter. You need will-power and a great deal of patience.

We have discussed taking full responsibility for the problem. Now ask yourself a few searching questions. Are you willing to sell some of your assets to get yourself out of debt? Would you sell your car? Would you sell your home if you had to? I am not suggesting here that all or any of these steps are actually going to be necessary, but you may as well be prepared to face up to the eventuality if needs dictate. If your case really is that pressing, then be assured that it is better for you to call the tune yourself than for the bank or other creditors to take the initiative. They do not, indeed cannot, have the same degree of interest in your affairs. It is up to you to remain in control.

Chapter Three

Money: a curious commodity

We all know someone – not us of course – who is absolutely useless with money. Try as he might, his financial affairs are a swirling undercurrent, chaotically undermining any prospect of a return to the black. To put him in charge of a piggy-bank, let alone cheque book and credit cards, might be seen to be the action of a deranged mind. Such a person may have been hovering on the verge of financial disaster for years, probably unaware that his only means of support in the world is an overdraft to which, somehow, the bank manager always agrees. The manager lives for the happy day when that promised, but never realised, bonus or slice of profit share will restore his client's affairs to order. So, in the meantime, he throws money at his client and his client throws money back at him, in the form of interest and administration charges. But as the overdraft becomes overdrawn so a cash advance on the credit card is provided to reduce it. Then the client finds that he cannot afford to pay the credit card bills, and the gas and electricity accounts are overdue. Back to the bank, this time for a consolidation loan to clear all the credit cards and other debts. This time our friend really does intend to walk the straight and narrow, but finds himself only three months later sitting across from the bank manager again. When he requests the extension of a modest overdraft facility, he may at last find that he is not well received, and that the manager points him firmly towards the door.

Perhaps, for the first time, our friend has been told 'No', and that leaves him with a number of questions – does he close his account and transfer his indebtedness to another unsuspecting bank manager? Does he blame the 'system' for his situation? Does he pray for a miracle or hold his head in despair? Or does he, at last, tackle the problem head on?

Anxiety and depression

Whatever the causes of your debt, anxiety and/or depression are the almost inescapable consequences. The symptoms may be obvious or hidden or may even require medical attention and drug therapy to bring them under control. The more you focus on the problem, the worse it seems to become and the less efficient you are in solving it. A 'catch-22' situation develops: is debt the cause of depression or has the depression caused the worsening debt? Only you can answer that truthfully, though it is probably accurate to suggest that a little bit of both is responsible.

However, there are some circumstances which can trigger debt and depression simultaneously: divorce is one example. Splitting up is not only often extremely depressing but can also have adverse financial consequences. The ex-husband may have to bear the cost of running two households for a while, or the ex-wife may have insufficient money to provide for the children when the ex-husband's earnings are low. While it is true that not all divorces are depressing, indeed they can be a great source of relief, they too can be undermined by new financial anxiety and depression which can so quickly set in.

Example 1

□ A married man with four children became so worked up over his financial difficulties that he had a complete breakdown. Gradually, the anxiety prompted by his money worries distorted his perception of reality until he irrationally feared that his family would have to be taken into care because he could not provide for them. Of course there was no danger whatsoever of this happening. Sadly, the man who had perfectly adequately provided for his family for 15 years was unable to share his fears with his wife, worried that she would reject him. His fears led him to an unhealthy introversion, and eventually to a breakdown, from which he needed hospital treatment to recover.

● Had this man been able to discuss his feelings with someone much earlier, the whole sad episode would probably have been avoided. After this experience, however, he learned to handle anxiety in a different way. He worked more reasonable hours, spent more time with his family and involved his wife much more closely in the family budget.

The only productive kind of anxiety, so far as debt is concerned, is that which prompts you to take the necessary steps towards putting your affairs in order. All other kinds of anxiety are useless. They will cloud your judgement, make you bad-tempered and leave you feeling constantly nervous about your problem. And that is hardly a strong position from which to fight. Anxious people do not exude confidence or encourage willing co-operation from creditors. On the contrary, creditors are much more likely to refuse you help if they suspect you are not quite stable. Of course, it is not easy to look in control when your world seems to be falling apart, but there are techniques you can develop to relieve anxiety.

Depression

Depression is by no means an easy state to define, and, depending on the severity of the symptons, can be difficult to treat. One of the saddest aspects of having financial problems (though it applies in countless other circumstances) is that they are almost always accompanied by depression. Many people feel as though they are trapped, with nowhere or no-one to turn to. They feel engulfed by their problems and turn in on themselves, swallowed in a 'blackness' which prevents them from tackling their difficulties realistically. They become so desperate that they will seek almost any escape route. And since the problem is often not just one but a number of debts, they end up taking out loan after loan, each to repay the other. Sadly, such debtors often fall prey to unscrupulous lenders who, mindful of the weakness of their client's position, exploit them to the full. It is hardly surprising, therefore, that some debtors require medical treatment, involving anti-depressant drugs, while the tragic few resort to suicide.

Such extreme depression tells us a great deal about the importance we place on money or, more properly, the lifestyles which we think can be bought with it. In our consumer society, we tend to equate our own worth with the range and quality of our material possessions. Advertising in particular pedals a lifestyle which, though thought desirable by the majority can be afforded only by the few. The ease, however, with which anyone can obtain credit, regardless of income and other commitments, gives rise to the illusion that the 'good life' is available to all. The problem lies in the mistaken assumption that more credit necessarily means more of the best. It is hardly surprising that when credit is suddenly seen for what it really is – 'debt' – those who are out of their depth with it often plunge into deep depression.

Depression, in severe cases, is extremely debilitating. Sufferers feel drained of energy (unlike anxiety which can induce an excess of it) both physically and mentally, causing a drop in work performance, accompanied by feelings of inadequacy. A few depressives even turn to drink and/or drugs to mask the symptoms and provide the impetus to carry on.

Taking the stress out of debt

If you have let your finances slip for whatever reason, then the chances are that you will have neglected other areas of your life. It is useless to apply the techniques for solving your financial problem without acknowledging and dealing with the fact that you got yourself into debt for a reason. If you do not tackle both the symptoms and the cause, you could easily end up in debt again.

First, you should think about all the possible causes for this predicament. Are you unemployed or unable to work through ill-health, or has a spouse given up work to look after the children? Have you been reckless with your money? – you may as well admit it to yourself now, as it will have to be acknowledged sooner or later.

Buy yourself an A4-sized notepad for recording all your thoughts and the action you are going to take. You will use this pad to discover the precise state of your affairs. You will also need an elementary filing system. An excellent and inexpensive system, which can be bought from large stationers, is the heavy duty cardboard expanding-wallet type, with pockets in alphabetical, chronological and numerical order. Next, you will need three office trays, and a good stock of erasers and correction fluid to work it out all over again if you make mistakes.

First, we are going to discover why you are in debt. You may believe your problem is caused by your not earning enough money to cover your expenses. But, being human, you will probably concede that you are occasionally prone to an exaggerated sense of your real financial needs. This first exercise may prove it.

Self-analysis chart

Rule a line down the centre of page one and head the left-hand column 'Why I am in debt'. Now make a list of all the possible reasons why you think you are in debt, regardless of how trivial or outlandish they may seem, or indeed, how terrifying the truth may be. This is possibly the first time you have ever sat down to confront the problem so do not be surprised if you find it very difficult. This is nothing to worry about. For the moment your mind simply does not want to face up to the reality of the situation. Take comfort, though. It may not be as bad as you have been dreading, and if it is, it will not seem quite so awful once you have begun to order your affairs. Understand that this exercise will relieve the spiralling irrational thoughts and worries that daily haunt you. The simple act of bringing your problems into the open will make you feel a lot better.

Example 2 shows a number of reasons why people think that they are in debt. It does not matter if you cannot think of all the reasons now. There is no point in giving yourself a headache so come back to it later if you are stuck – it may take several days before you complete this list. In the meanwhile, be assured that you have set the wheels of progress in motion. It may not seem to be much of an achievement, but you will soon see how valuable is this exercise. As your mind becomes accustomed to thinking about debt in a constructive way, you will find that the solutions to your problems may not be as remote as you once thought. Try to distance yourself from any emotional attachment or assessment of your problem as you make the list. For the moment, at least, this is simply an intellectual exercise.

Example 2

WHY I AM IN DEBT
Unemployed
Wages too low
Outgoings too high
All the bills came at once
Took a loan I couldn't really afford
Spend too much on clothes
Last year's holiday cost a fortune – still paying the credit card bill
School fees – didn't budget for them
Death/illness in the family
Divorce
Didn't get expected pay rise
Running costs of car
Eat out too often
Can't control my spending
Always buying things for the children
State benefit not enough
Assessed for tax unpaid
Drink too much
Gambling too much

Now that you have owned up to all the grisly facts surrounding your debt problem, why not treat yourself in some small way – make a special effort with a dinner, or take some time out with the family. And here is something else you might like to consider as part of your recovery programme. When did you last do any regular exercise? Exercise helps reduce tension, anxiety and can even take the edge off depression. And once you start eliminating a depressed, 'there's nothing I can do' state of mind, the sooner you can begin to tackle your financial problems successfully.

The next obvious but perhaps painful task is to list what can be done to improve the situation opposite each of these headings. Approach each problem separately and objectively.

Chapter Four

You can make it (if you really want to)

You have already done some important work in discovering the reasons why you are in debt, and thinking about ways to approach the symptoms positively. Now look again at the chart, comparing your suggested remedies with those in example below.

SELF-ANALYSIS CHART

Why I am in debt	**What can I do about it?**
Unemployed	Could research the possible options for retraining and perhaps learn new skills, for example in electronics or computing. That way I might stand a better chance of a good job in the future. In the meantime, talk to creditors and try to get them to help by accepting lower repayments for a while.
Last year's holiday cost a fortune – still paying the credit card bill	If this really is a drain on cash-flow, ask the bank for a loan to repay the balance outstanding on the credit cards. Banks will normally allow 12 months for holiday loans to be repaid, however, this can be extended in special circumstances.
Assessed for tax unpaid	Write to the Inland Revenue asking for more time to pay. They will normally allow up to two years for 'back-tax' to be repaid, as long as the payments are made regularly. They will also usually accept an arrangement where your tax code is reduced for a period of time, until the debt is paid. This means they collect the money at source, and you do not have to worry about trying

to remember whether you missed a payment. The taxman will try to be as helpful as possible, as long as you admit liability (if their sums are correct!) and intend to pay. Tax evasion can lead to court proceedings.

It is surprising how impotent many people feel when trying to find an answer to their debt problems. They feel daunted by the size and apparent power of their creditors – as if they are just waiting for you to default so they can come and repossess your home and belongings. By completing the 'What I can do about it' section of the chart, you will see that the emphasis is on seeking advice and/or negotiating with creditors. The examples given are but a few of the many options available.

The major point of the exercise is to get you thinking about how *you* would go about settling your debts. Your answers will tell you a lot about your lifestyle. Are you too extravagant with your money? What are your priorities and are you being realistic with the answers you have given? Realism is a key ingredient to financial stability. Call it self-discipline, thrift or plain common sense, if you have not got it yet, you will have learned it by the time you have finished reading this book. Keep referring to your chart. You may find other things to add to it from time to time but, most importantly, it is your confessional, which you can either keep to yourself, or share with a trusted second party.

An imaginative way out

Although it is very important to be realistic and positive in your thoughts and actions when tackling your debt, there is no harm at all in using a little imagination to spur you on. You must have wondered, for instance, what life would be like if you were not saddled with all those pressing demands for payment. You should understand that imagination plays a very important part in decision making, sometimes persuading us that a purchase is essential when it really is not so. Beware the advertisers who pander to this presenting images of desirable objects or places using flawless film stars and personalities to sell us all too often what we do not really need and perhaps cannot afford. Try the following exercise.

On a fresh page in your notebook write down your present income (net take home pay) in the top left corner. Now write down the following headings:

NET PAY

If I had no debts
could I afford . . . ?

	YES/NO		YES/NO
To get a mortgage		Christmas presents	
To pay rent		Birthday presents	
To pay rates		The theatre/opera/ballet	
Buildings insurance		Pub	
Contents insurance		Cinema	
Mortgage protection insurance		Restaurant	
		Flea market	
Furniture		Antique shop	
Washing machine		Junk shop	
Cooker		Children's savings	
Dish washer		Art gallery	
Kitchen equipment		Concerts	
Weekly food		Stereo equipment	
Weekly entertainment		Video	
The clothes I like		Television	
A holiday		Records	
To run a car		Tapes	
Life insurance		Exhibitions	
Medical insurance		Books	
Private pension fund		Make-up	
School fees		Sweets	
Clothes for the children		Children's treats	
Jewellery		Fares to work	
Tea rooms		Plants	
Hairdressers		Health care	
		Sports equipment	

First go through the list, ticking off 'Yes' or 'No' against the items you consider essential. Next, tick those which appeal to you most. Feel free to add anything else not shown. Then re-write your lists in order of priority, with a figure of estimated cost against each heading. Remember, you are using your imagination, but you are also constrained by your real income. Add up the total cost of all your items and compare it with your income. How far out are you? Indeed, does your income allow you to have or provide for only the essential items such as mortgage, rates and fuel bills, plus some food; or are your earnings adequate to satisfy more than that? It is a fairly confident predicition that you could not afford much more than the basic essentials on your list. The choice you now have is this: 1. Do I go without everything else? 2. Do I go into debt for some of it? or 3. Do I go into debt for the lot? Look long and hard at your list, and make a rational decision about what is essential.

If you were a book-keeper or accountant, working on behalf of a client, you would scrupulously manage their finances. You would not permit indulgence or spending beyond what was necessary for the efficient running of the business and the comfort of staff. You know full well that if you did, the business would fold rapidly. Now apply this principle to your own list. Cut out everything which is superfluous to your wellbeing, allowing, of course, a little margin for entertainment and personal spending.

The idea is not to turn you into a cave-dwelling recluse, but to see what you can make do with while still leading a comfortable life. Now, are you still in debt? If so, by how much? Remember, you are the sole arbiter of what you think is necessary for you (and your family) to live on. Make a note of your debt figure and divide it by 12 or 52, depending on whether you are paid monthly or weekly. Do you think you could afford to pay off this debt from your total family income, or would you need an overdraft and other loans to manage? Play around with the figures and items on the list until you have found the most acceptable compromise.

Since all of this was imaginary, compare your list with your present situation and see if there are similarities in either your wants or your debts. You may be surprised to learn, perhaps, that your make-believe financial adviser was kinder with your money than you are in reality. He was given clear-cut choices to deal with and probably showed no hesitation in reaching decisions based on acceptable compromise.

It was not so difficult to imagine on paper an ideal financial position, given the constraints of income. Why not then, adopt this plan in real life? There is absolutely no reason for you to assume that this cannot be done. If you need more convincing evidence of this, just take a look around you at all the shops and enterprises on your doorstep. Without exception, they started from nothing – except, that is, an idea, the product of someone's imagination. Plans were made, professionals consulted and cash raised. If the plans and financial forecasts are wildly out, the business fails. On the other hand, if most of the plans and forecasts are nearly always correct, then, the business succeeds. There is nothing magical about it: just commonsense, a little imagination and a lot of hard work.

Your own financial affairs are very similar to that of any business. You earn money for work done, and you have to provide a system for paying creditors – the gas, electricity and phone boards, for example, and the building society. And just as a business pays its employees, so you have to ensure that each member of the household has sufficient spending money. A business, if it is well run and wishes to survive, must also make one vital provision: an accounting system to monitor the flow of cash and to help you decide which creditors get paid first and who, inevitably, has to wait.

That is where the similarities end for, surprisingly, few people have a day-to-day method of cash management and certainly no system of recording payments and when they are due. Most rely on last month's bank statement to inform them of what they already know, that they have spent too much, but they learn little about why all the money disappeared. They are constantly back-tracking, searching through drawers full of old credit card slips, dog-eared bills and unopened, 'official-looking' envelopes. By the time they think they have made some sense of last month's mess, this month's is upon them; and the whole agonising process is repeated, again and again.

Chapter Five

The balancing act

If you have been stuffing unopened buff-coloured envelopes inside a drawer because you feel unable to face up to the contents, the time has come to take a deep breath and recover them from their hiding place. You are going to have to face up to the whole ghastly truth. You will never know the full extent of your problem until you work out, blow by blow, every single item of expenditure and income in your household.

If you have children old enough to understand what is going on, do try to involve them; not only will they help take the edge off the work, they might come up with some good ideas themselves. But be sure that you do not pass on your own worst fears to them. Children can be easily scared and, just like adults, can plunge into a nightmare world full of irrational and terrifying worries. They need security, so do not let them think that your whole world is collapsing. Just let them see that extra care is needed.

You will need to find all your bills, bank statements, hire-purchase agreements, and your regular weekly or monthly receipts. If, like most people, you do not keep itemised receipts from the supermarket, start now. Dig out all your garage bills, car insurance policy, break-down membership subscription and expenditure on tools. Turn to p.63 and check off your expenditure against the chart, adding any others that may apply. If you cannot find details of everything at once, do not worry, it will probably take a few days to piece everything together. If some records are totally lost, telephone the creditor or payee and ask what was the last amount you paid or is owing now. If you feel too embarrassed, ashamed or nervous about making contact with them, think about this – you have come too far now to pretend that there is no difficulty. Until you know the exact amount of money owing, you will not be able to carry out the rest of the exercises in this book.

As we established you must take responsibility for the problem and resolve it, no matter what. Your financial mess is going to get better, by degrees. With persistence and the will to win you can start to make some important inroads into your debt, and that can only help restore your self-confidence and the confidence of your creditors in you. The next exercise is probably the hardest you will encounter in this work, and you may have to tackle it gradually, or with your partner.

Chart One

ESSENTIAL MONTHLY OUTGOINGS

Item	**Amount**	**Date due**	**Amount outstanding**
Mortgage			
Rent			
Mortgage/Rent arrears			
Second mortgage			
Second mortgage arrears			
Rates			
Rate arrears			
Water rates			
Water rate arrears			
Maintenance payments			
Court fines			
Gas			
Electricity			
Telephone			
Total	£		£

All the items listed on Chart One are those that could land you in greater trouble if they are not paid. Obviously, if you do not keep up the mortgage payments, you can expect to be evicted sooner or later. Non-payment of rates and rate arrears could land you in jail as will non-payment of court fines. The water authority can disconnect you for arrears and prosecute as well. The gas and electricity boards can disconnect and take you to court to recover any arrears. Finally, if you default on maintenance payments to a former partner, you could go to prison.There may be other things essential to you, a telephone for example. However, it is not included in our chart because its absence does not present a threat to life or liberty; although British Telecom can sue for non-payment in addition to disconnecting the line. Similarly, a television is not essential, though if you have one, you must have a licence or else face heavy fines or even imprisonment.

Add up the total monthly amount owing in the left-hand column and also the total debt outstanding. For example, your monthly mortgage payment may be £200, but the amount you owe on your home may be £30,000. Put this figure in the right hand column. When calculating monthly expenditure on gas and electricity, try to find bills covering the past 12 months. Add them up and divide by 12 to give you a monthly average figure. If you only have the last quarter's bill to hand, divide it by 3 to give an average. Apply this formula to all the other items until you have filled in both columns, one for monthly expenses, the other for total outstanding. Now, put this pile of demands in one of your trays with 'Chart One' on top. Label this tray 'Essential Monthly Outgoings'.

The list of items in Chart Two (below) may be incomplete, but you will know from your personal circumstances what has been omitted.

Most people go shopping on a weekly basis, so to find the monthly total, simply multiply your weekly bills by 4 (or 4.3 to be exact). You may be surprised to see bank loans, overdrafts, credit cards and HP lumped together in this list. As long as you have not used your home as collateral you have no fear of eviction. In the case of credit cards, they are in no way secured on your property. The only way you could lose your home is if your total debts exceed £750 to each creditor in which case, under the law, you can be bankrupted (see page 105). However, at this stage, it is not a possibility you need fear.

As with Chart One, add up the totals and put these documents in another wire tray labelled 'Important Weekly/Monthly Outgoings'. Put 'Chart Two' on the top.

Chart Two

IMPORTANT WEEKLY/MONTHLY OUTGOINGS

Item		**Amount**	**Date due**	**Amount outstanding**
Food and Housekeeping				
Bank loans (unsecured)	1.			
	2.			
	3.			
Overdraft (unsecured)				
Hire purchase				
Credit-sale				
Credit cards	1.			
	2.			
	3.			
In-store cards				
Home insurance				
Life insurance				
Pension plan				
Television licence				
Telephone				
Car: fuel and oil				
Fares to work				
Mail order catalogues (list each one)				
Milk				
Pet food				
Total	£			£

Next, let us examine all the other outgoings which may be classed as essential but periodic payments. Some of these would be immediate targets for cutback or elimination. When you have completed this list, put all the bills and receipts in a tray labelled 'Other Periodic Outgoings' and put 'Chart Three' on top.

Chart Three

OTHER PERIODIC OUTGOINGS

Item	**Amount**	**Date due**
Ground rent		
Car: tax		
insurance		
MOT		
Garage bills		
TV rental		
Video rental		
Clothing		
General repairs		
Christmas presents		
Book club		
Record club		
Birthday presents		
School fees		
Alcohol		
Tobacco		
Subscriptions		
Sundry items		
Total	£	

Analysing Chart One – Essential Outgoings

You now have to decide who is going to be paid first. This priority is determined by the rights your creditors have, either to your property or to your liberty. The other relevant factor concerns the efficiency of the organisation to whom you owe money. In other words, some creditors will be more persistent in their demands than others. This does not mean that you can, or will in any way avoid paying your debts; you are simply going to use whatever leeway you have to help you back on course. It is a fact of business life that those who shout loudest, and longest, get paid first.Every business has a priority list of creditors, and that means some have to wait until there is sufficient cash-flow in the business to pay everyone. This is broadly how you are going to approach your own problem, using skilful diplomacy and the art of negotiation.

Mortgage

Most people would agree that keeping a roof over their heads is the single most important concern in their lives. Since the home is also potentially an excellent investment, it is vital that you do not lose it.

The building society, bank or finance company who lent you the money to buy your home are fully secured creditors, that is to say, your loan is tied to the property, so you either pay the mortgage and keep the home, or stop paying and lose it. This payment takes absolute precedence over all others and comes, therefore, at the top of the list. If you have taken out a second mortgage for home improvements then this too is tied to your home, and if you are in arrears the lender (mortgagee) has certain rights in law to seek possession. If you have a second mortgage from a different lender, be sure to contact him swiftly if you are in difficulties. We will be dealing with this in chapter seven.

Rent

Whether public or private, tenants can be evicted for non-payment of rent and arrears. It is easy to understand how some tenants withhold the rent because a large or unexpected bill arrives which has to be paid. Often, this unofficial 'credit' helps many people to make ends meet. Provided the arrears are paid with the full rent next time, it is doubtful that the landlord would do anything other than remonstrate with you. However, persistent failure to pay rent, along with rent arrears, will eventually leave you homeless as the landlord will serve a notice to quit, and you can then be evicted by a magistrate. Paying the rent then, is as important as keeping up the mortgage.

Rates

Few people would claim they get real value for money from the rates that they pay, and many would rather withhold payment altogether. Yet they do so at their peril, for the General Rate is a tax levied on property ownership by central government, which requires the local authority to collect it. If it cannot do so, or you fail to pay voluntarily, then you will receive a distress warrant from the bailiff's office. If you do not comply with its terms, the local authority can seize your goods to the value of the amount of rates outstanding, plus costs. If you do not have sufficient assets to cover the debt, or hide them or give them away, you will probably go to gaol. After mortgage or rent, the rates are second in importance.

Maintenance payments

The tripwires in the minefield of separation, divorce and maintenance are many and varied. An errant spouse can suffer heavily by failing to keep up agreed payments. An ex-wife can ask the court to issue a Warrant of Execution on the husband, which permits the bailiff to enter his home and seize goods to the value of the arrears. Other than this, the wife can ask for a Judgement Summons from either the county or high court. A formal court hearing must take place and, providing that the wife or her representatives can prove the case for arrears, the husband can be sent to prison.

Court fines

There are many reasons why you might have a court fine. For example, you may not have paid the last parking ticket, hoping to escape the system. Ultimately, though, you can be sent to prison for non-payment of *any* fine, although the courts would probably be reluctant to gaol you for a parking offence. If however, you have been fined for non-payment of car tax or other petty offences, and cannot or will not pay, you will receive a distress warrant and can expect the bailiff to pay a visit unless you settle the debt quickly.

Gas/Electricity/Telephone

These creditors are at the bottom of the list of priority payments, not because you can necessarily go without these utilities, but because it is nearly always easier to compromise with these creditors than a court. If you are one of the millions who wait until the bill actually arrives without budgeting for it, then you are going to have to learn new habits quickly, in order to make fuel bill panic a thing of the past.

Summary

With luck, some of the confusion has been taken out of who should be paid first. We are now going to move on to charts Two and Three, tackling them in the same way. By the time this exercise is completed, you will have the beginnings of your personal budget, or your 'financial barometer' showing the peaks and troughs of your income and expenditure, and putting you back in control of your spending. But before we leave chart one, sift through all the documents in the tray and mark down on the chart the due date of each payment. In the case of fuel bills, finish chapter six before filling in this part.

Analysing Chart Two – Important Weekly/Monthly Outgoings

Food and housekeeping

This section could arguably head the list of essential outgoings. The reason why it appears here is because you have direct control over how much you spend on food and can, in some ways, cut your coat according to your cloth. For example, is there any point in supporting your local corner shop if baked beans and butter cost 5p or 10p more than the supermarket? All those forays to the corner shop probably cost a fortune. How many times have you just gone down the road for eggs and bread and come back with a basket-load of unessential extras?

The most economical way to shop is first of all to prepare a list of all the essential items that you need per week. By all means, add a few treats for yourself or the children, but do be realistic about this: children won't die or wither away without their usual quota of sweets and chocolate. A few carefully chosen items could cost a lot less and do far more good. If you are not in the habit of making lists, you may be surprised at just how few things are really essential. Try to set aside one day a week for your shopping and stick to that day. Arrange it so that you are not under any pressure to be elsewhere at the time, otherwise your attention may be so distracted that you end up slipping into the bad old ways. Try to adhere to your list as far as possible, but do not deprive yourself of something essential for the sake of being a martyr. The idea is to build a good stock of essential foods at home so that you do not have to dash out on panic buying sprees every two or three days.

Once you have established a routine of weekly shopping, you may be pleasantly surprised at the time as well as money you save by adopting this particular discipline. By the way, all those 'money-off' tokens you find on washing powder and a host of other products can contribute quite a lot to cutting your food bill, so do keep them.

People with similar incomes may have very different ideas about diet and nutrition, and how much they should spend on food. Although one family may spend twice as much as the next, it does not mean that they are going to be twice as healthy. It is sensible, therefore, to cultivate an interest in food, to find out what is nutritious and what is bad for you.

Bank loans (unsecured)

An example of an unsecured loan is borrowing to buy something such as hi-fi equipment or perhaps a car, when you are not asked to use your home as security for the loan. However, if you default, the bank can still sue you for the outstanding amount,which could involve bailiffs and seizure of goods in lieu. All this means court judgements against you, which will prejudice your future chances of borrowing until the judgements are discharged.

Overdrafts

These are almost always unsecured because most overdrafts are short-term, repayable by a due date, which can be altered with the agreement of the bank. However, an overdraft might be secured if the sum borrowed is very large and there is no clear time span during which it is to be repaid. Overdrafts can be called in on demand too, so it is important to ensure that you make some progress in paying it back, no matter how little you can afford on a weekly/monthly basis.

Hire purchase

No so popular these days, hire purchase is a legal agreement between you and a finance company, not the shop where you bought the goods. You cannot sell them until you have paid the last instalment, and if you default, the finance company can repossess them, subject to satisfying certain conditions. Since interest rates are usually high it is wise to pay back these loans as quickly as possible. See chapters six, seven and eight.

Credit-sale

Not to be confused with hire purchase, credit-sale agreements transfer ownership of the goods to you, even though you still have to pay a finance company, (not the shop where you bought them), regular instalments.

Many of the large multiple electrical and retailing outlets are licensed credit brokers nowadays, and so, in effect, you are dealing with 'the shopkeeper' on certain occasions. Once again, interest rates for credit-sale are high, so pay off the debt as soon as you can. See chapters six, seven and eight.

Credit cards

These 'flexible friends' which will 'do nicely' anywhere, are a hugely popular method of spreading the cost of a large purchase over several payments. The problem is that credit cards are being used more and more frequently as a second source of income because cash advances are readily available up to the maximum of your credit limit. Although interest rates tend to be somewhat lower than for in-store cards, allowing interest to accrue can be extremely expensive in the long run. It is therefore wise to keep a weather eye on credit card spending – when you end up buying the toothpaste and toilet paper with them, you know something is wrong! See chapters six, seven and eight.

This brings to a close all the debts over which you have little or no control. In Chart One, all the debts were totally essential, otherwise you would have no roof over your head, and if you did, nothing to heat your home or cook your food. In Chart Two, the debts outlined are essential, although there is some debate as to how necessary they really are. Having taken them on, however, you no longer have the luxury of choosing to repay them – the consequences are grim if you do not. The rest of Chart Two deals with optional debts, although you may consider them essential to your lifestyle.

In-store cards

These often go under the guise of budget cards or budget accounts, and there are hundreds of different goods which can be bought with them, from hi-fi and micro-electronics to clothes and food. It would be virtually impossible for most goods available with this method of purchase to be repossessed, so, once again, ownership is transferred to the buyer at the time of purchase. Interest rates are usually very high for the privilege, and so these accounts should be cleared quickly. See chapters six, seven and eight.

Home insurance

It would be bad advice and a false economy in the extreme to suggest scrapping your home contents policy.

It is therefore worthwhile checking your policy details against your present circumstances. Are you over-insured? Has a member of the family recently left, taking a large proportion of what is covered under your policy? The saving may not be large, but it will certainly help towards paying off something that is urgent, for example an up-to-the-limit credit card.

Life insurance

This is a totally optional commitment, though it is sometimes hard to believe that this is the case with all the compelling newspaper and television advertising campaigns. Your policy may provide cover for 'life' only, or there may be some cash value if your life insurance is also a savings plan, depending on how long you have been paying premiums. There may even be an option to borrow against the eventual cash value of the policy. It all very much depends on which kind of insurance you have or are thinking about. If you want to ensure that your dependants will be adequately provided for in the event of your early death, a 'joint-life, first-death' policy could be the answer. You have the choice of whether you want a payout on maturity or just life insurance, the latter obviously being cheaper.

If you are seriously thinking of saving money through cutting back on life insurance though, it would be wise to speak to your broker before reaching any decision.

Pension plan

For those who can afford them, pension plans offer the possibility of financial stability from retirement through to old age. A good plan will almost certainly have a built-in option to borrow against the eventual cash value of the plan, together with life insurance cover. For the self-employed, pension plans are becoming increasingly attractive in that, currently, up to 17½% of gross income can be ploughed into the scheme. There are tax benefits too, which any accountant should be able to secure. If you are already paying into a private pension scheme and are finding that you could do without this extra financial responsibility, then you may well discover that you can temporarily 'freeze' the policy until times are better. You then pick up where you left off, with little or no loss of retirement benefit. You do not have to be self-employed to pay into a pension scheme. Many employers are affiliated with one of the major funds, and this may be the source of your future retirement income. However, there is nothing preventing you from taking on another, providing no more than 17½% of your gross income goes into all schemes. At the moment however, in the context of this book, you are probably not in the desirable position of having two private pension incomes, and maybe not even one.

Television licence

Once again, this is something which most probably you would rather not have to pay; however, the television licensing authority in Bristol is becoming quite efficient at tracking down offenders and bringing them to book. So the advice, if you haven't got one yet is to get one soon, or get rid of the television (an even more effective economy!). Punishment is severe – up to £400 fine and even imprisonment.

Telephone

British Telecom has around 17 million private customers so, arguably, the telephone is as essential as all the other items discussed. If you are self-employed, infirm or elderly,the telephone is probably absolutely necessary. For the rest of us, though, it is conceivably something that we could do without in the short term. Do not forget that telephone calls are not cheap – just check your local directory or call-charge information booklet to see how much they cost. There are three types of call charge relating to the different times of the day and the day of the week, and these are explained in detail in your code book.

Getting the most from your telephone requires a little planning. Do you really have to make all your calls to friends during peak rate times, or can they wait until later? Can you get people to call you back, instead of 'hanging-on' for them? Leave messages on answer-phones instead of hanging up in fright at having to speak to the wretched thing – it will save you money. If you have no idea what the current call charges are, dial 100 and ask for Freefone 2500. You will receive a leaflet detailing the local and national rates.

If you use the telephone a great deal, it may be worthwhile considering a 'money-box' telephone. This is a desk-top model which takes coins of most denominations. It also tells you how much you have used during a particular call, the total in the money box, the time of day and a number of other things. Rental charges for these systems are high by comparison with normal telephones, about £23 as opposed to £14 per quarter, so you should have a good reason for installing one in the first place. At least the bill you receive will be paid for out of the proceeds of the money box – provided you don't cheat!

Car fuel and oil

Does your car return satisfactory miles per gallon or have you no idea how much fuel it consumes? For around £15 most four cylinder models can be tuned and have the exhaust gases analysed.Even a saving of five miles a gallon could soon add up to considerable savings at the petrol pump.

Perhaps you could also consider car sharing.Are there people in your area who work at the same place or near to you? You could cut your own fuel costs quite dramatically by sharing the costs with colleagues or neighbours.

Fares to work

You cannot do much about the cost of public transport except to change your method of travelling. Over the past few years a thriving industry has been built upon disillusioned rail travellers. Air-conditioned, luxury coaches take you to your destination in style and more cheaply than the train. Investigate the coach options in your area – you may be very pleasantly surprised at the difference. Otherwise a car-share scheme might be in operation in your area, or you could start one yourself. If you live close enough, how about cycling to work instead, getting fitter at the same time.

Mail order catalogues

If you use this method for a lot of your clothes buying, how about becoming an agent yourself? The formalities are few and the benefits considerable when you spend a fair amount. You receive commission, normally 10% on all purchases, paid out in monthly cheques. Many mail order firms operate interest-free credit terms, which can be useful when considering a large purchase such as a washing machine or dish washer. Why pay interest on a credit card or budget account when you can buy the same goods for less and have a longer repayment period? The list of goods available from catalogues is nowadays very comprehensive and worth investigating.

As with other debts though, you should be careful not to let your spending get out of control. Set a limit which you know you can afford to repay, and keep to it until the outstanding balance has been reduced considerably. Some catalogues operate 'add to' terms which, on the surface, look very attractive. It seems that the more you spend, the less your monthly repayments are under the scheme. This, of course, does not alter the fact that you owe a lot of money – regardless of how long you have to pay and how small the instalments.

Pet food

A popular brand of catfood can cost 10p more than the same brand at the supermarket. The cat eats about five tins per week which, if bought from the corner shop, costs more than six tins from the supermarket. The same goes for the dog. The savings to be made by buying once a week from the supermarket is in the region of £70 per year for the two animals; not a fantastic saving perhaps, but significant when combined with a wide range of other possible savings.

Milk

It may be hard to think of saving when it comes to milk, but in fact it is cheaper to order from the milkman instead of buying from shops.

Analysing Chart Three – Other Periodic Outgoings

Items in this category are generally those over which you have greatest control since most of them, apart from medical bills and obligatory payments such as ground rent, are subjective choices, initiated perhaps in better times. The most obvious candidates for cutback occur in this group. So, once again, please note them down on your list.

Car: tax/insurance/MOT

The problem with cars – or maybe those who own them – is that once you have one it is very difficult to give it up. As a nation we lavish millions on the upkeep of these tin symbols of freedom and status. There is nothing wrong with this of course, provided that you can afford it. A visiting Dane once remarked that if we took as much pride in our homes and environment as we do in our cars, England would be so much more attractive. Perhaps he did not realise at the time that the cost of cars and their upkeep is less than one third of that in Denmark. Nonetheless, he does have a point because the cost of keeping a car on the road relative to the average wage is very high. How much could you save by not having one? If your finances are in a mess this could be one way of making a tremendous saving. You should, at any rate, consider changing your current model for a smaller, more economical one.

When did you last shop around for insurance quotations for your car? Are you sure that you have the best cover at the most competitive rate? Although it is difficult to understand why, insurance premiums for identical models vary widely,sometimes by hundreds of pounds from broker to broker. Be sure to keep your broker on his toes by checking out the market from time to time. Most firms have easy payment facilities today, enabling you to spread the cost of insurance over a full year, although you will have to pay a little extra for the privilege. This does at least release valuable cash which would otherwise be accounted for by the car.

The only instalment system for car tax involves paying it half-yearly instead of annually. At current rates this will cost £55 every six months rather than £100 for the year, however, if you rearrange your car insurance, you should be able to start saving now for your next tax disc.

It is of course, illegal to drive a car without a current MOT certificate. Although the test fee is not very expensive (around £11.50), the garage bill for labour and parts could exceed this figure by many times if you do not service your car regularly, and have the bodywork and chassis checked for rust and structural defects.

Garage bills

Car repairs and maintenance can be a licence to print money for the garage owner and mechanics if you are careless and do not tie them down to a firm quotation for any proposed work. Most will provide an estimate subject to their not finding any other faults in the process, which you are almost always told about after the event, when the bill is presented. Always ask what the current labour rate is and whether parts are charged out at cost to you, or are 'marked up' by the garage, to increase their own profit on the work. Get two or three quotes for

the job before committing yourself and ensure there will be no hidden extras.
Be sure to stick to the service intervals recommended by the manufacturer; skipping a service is nearly always a false economy, often ending in high repair bills for damage done as a result some time in the future. Avoid the 'cowboy' mechanic who gives no guarantee of his work. Some mechanics always provide the gloomiest prognosis of a car, lowering your expectations while increasing their profit for the job.The best recommendation is by word of mouth, perhaps through a friend who has had good service.

Television/video rental

The major television and video rental companies are currently locked in fierce competition for your business. There are a number of schemes on offer, designed to give better value for money and flexibility with equipment. On average, the cost of renting a television and video together is around £25 - £30 per month. After two years you would have spent more than enough to buy the equipment outright.

The only real advantage of renting is that the hirer is obliged to repair or replace faulty equipment at no extra cost to you. But if you bought outright in the first place, you could have an optional two or three year parts and labour warranty for a modest extra sum, so from the third year onwards, ownership must be the better option. Some electrical retailers are offering a 'lease/buy' package, whereby you rent the equipment for the first three years, at the end of which it becomes your property. It may sound fair, but just look at the interest rates charged for hiring the equipment and then compare them with the cost of a bank personal loan, enabling you to shop around for the best deal.

Most people would probably shrink from parting with the television, but what about the video, if you have one. Is it really necessary? After all a saving of £15-£20 per month is significant, and can be put to good use elsewhere in your budget. When your money is back on a proper footing, you can always buy/rent or lease once again; for the moment however, the video is the first thing to consider parting with.

Clothing

If you are a regular clothes buyer you will know how costly a varied wardrobe can be. Are clothes purchases responsible for those high interest credit-card instalments or budget accounts? Clothes are necessary, but you must be ruthlessly honest and realistic about whether you can afford them. Why not plan seasonal spending on clothes, keeping an eye out for the traditional sale periods and setting yourself a limit which you will not exceed. This way you can plan ahead and perhaps even save some cash towards your planned spending spree, instead of relying on the credit cards. Or, use the cards, taking full advantage of the interest-free period, and then settle the account in full (see chapter eight).

General repairs

These will be required periodically, even if you do not own your home. If you do, you must bear the full cost alone, unless the repair qualifies as an improvement – for example, installing a standard amenity such as a bath, washbasin with hot and cold water, and inside lavatory. In this case, a local authority grant towards the cost might be available. There are several types of grant for which you might qualify, though waiting lists can be extremely long. In any event, contact your local authority and ask them to send details of all grant aid available. They will also tell you how long the waiting list is (assuming you qualify for a grant). Household repairs can be left for only so long before they could become serious and expensive. The debt-buster budget (see page 63) will show you how to provide, partially at least, for these eventualities, taking the shock out of the repair bill.

If you are a tenant, the landlord will probably be responsible for all external repairs to the building and its boundaries, and also internal defects. Public tenants should have written agreements setting out the responsibilities of both landlord and tenant. If you do not have one, ask the landlord – it is your right. Housing law is complex and difficult to enforce as there is no single act of parliament embracing the subject. However, your local Citizen's Advice Bureau or Community Law Centre should be able to help in any dispute over home repairs or improvements, if the landlord is unwilling to carry them out.

Christmas presents

We would all love to give the children most of the things they want for Christmas. If you are in debt though, you have to be totally realistic. You cannot afford to put your recovery programme in peril because of December 25. Now is the time to tell your *adult* family and friends that you wish them a very merry Christmas but that you cannot exchange presents this year. Talk to your children. Explain to them clearly that you won't be able to give them so much but that instead you will take them to the cinema or zoo as a treat. They will understand and would rather see you being honest with them than watch you silently worry, becoming depressed.

Book/Record club

Millions of books, records, tapes and compact discs are sold through clubs, guilds or societies every year. The initial offer usually takes the form of goods at drastically reduced prices to induce your membership. You are then committed to buying at least two or three items per year, or more if you wish, all at specially discounted rates. You are sent periodic statements which you are supposed to settle on receipt. It is easy to run up quite large bills using this method, which amounts to interest-free credit. Nonetheless, the bill should be settled in full. If you are already in debt, another £20-£30 a month or quarter is a significant and unnecessary extra outlay which should be halted as soon as possible, so that these funds can be diverted into other more urgent areas. If you cannot meet these payments, then you must come to an arrangement with the organisation concerned. (See chapter 7.)

Birthday presents

The advice for these is exactly the same as for Christmas presents – do not unless you have to. No adult will expect a present (they haven't grown up if they do!), and so a tasteful card and message will do just as well. If yours is a large family with lots of nieces and nephews with birthdays every month of the year, buy only for the children, but find out from the parents in advance what they think would be well received. Books or records are always a safe bet and will not bankrupt you either. Nobody wants to feel they have cheated the children out of their presents, but it is far better to be honest about your situation than to go into debt for emotional reasons. Birthdays are once a year – your debt is with you all the time.

School fees

During this decade there has been a revival of the fee-paying public school system because many parents feel concerned about the alleged poor quality of state education. Whatever the pros and cons of private education, it costs a lot and should be planned very carefully before any commitment is made. Your bank or financial adviser will be able to tell you of any special savings plans and tax benefits available.

If your present situation indicates that you will no longer be able to afford a fee-paying school then you have some unenviable soul-searching to do. Your sense of obligation as a parent may outweigh all other financial and personal considerations, in which case you will need to examine the possibility of a second income, as well as reducing your outgoings. Perhaps you could sell some assets to cover the school fees for one more term or even a year. It will help, but you must find a way of generating enough money or cutting your expenditure so as to make a permanent difference to your affairs.

Alcohol/Tobacco

Taken in extreme moderation, tobacco and alcohol can help relieve the symptoms of stress and anxiety, probably without doing very much harm to health. The problem is defining 'in moderation'. For some, three cigarettes and a pint of beer a day may be adequate, while others require 20 cigarettes and five pints to achieve the same effect. Since financial worries can cause enormous stress and anxiety, smokers and/or drinkers will be tempted to increase their consumption.

Avoid this downward spiral, for not only will you be putting your health at greater risk, but you will also plunge deeper in debt to finance the habit, thus solving nothing. If you are one of those who feel unable to cut down or give up smoking and drinking at this time, then it would probably be psychologically unwise for you to consider this option at the moment since it would only create more unwanted stress. But by the same token, make a resolution not to increase your consumption either, especially if your intake is only very moderate.

If drink is the main cause of your financial problem, you owe it to yourself and family to seek professional help as soon as possible, otherwise you will not be able to solve your financial difficulties, let alone the underlying cause of your alcoholism. This is a big step to take, but can only help restore you to the real world and increase your self-esteem.

Subscriptions/sundry items

This really covers all the loose ends in your spending. For example, do you still have a bankers' order for a publication you hardly ever read but cannot be bothered to cancel? Is it really necessary to buy a newspaper every day of the week with the extensive television news coverage and Sunday bumper editions? Liquid lunches at work undoubtedly mount up in cost over the weeks and months. How about moderating this to once or twice a week, taking sandwiches to work and doing exercise during the lunch hour? It is a good bet that quite a lot of unnecessary spending on food/drink is the direct result of boredom at work or home.

This concludes the debit side of the equation. By now you should be used to raking over the details, dredging up the horrid truth about your finances. Are you in any way surprised at the amount of money you spend when all the foregoing information is taken into account, or were you expecting something like this? Either way, you have completed a valuable exercise which will be the cornerstone of your personal budget.

Now we are going to move on to the credit side to find if any of your assets can be converted to help you out of difficulties.

The three ways of tackling debt on the financial level are by reducing outlay, increasing income and by combining the two. It makes sense to explore the first possibility as fully as possible since clearly, it is easier to save than to have to work longer hours to earn more. Charts One to Three suggested ways of reducing outlay. But now take a look at Chart Four. This lists many of the traditional areas of household income – but are there ways in which you can increase this?

Chart Four

INCOME

Item	**Amount**
Wages/Salary (not including occasional overtime)	
Man	
Woman	
Unemployment benefit	
Supplementary benefit	
Invalidity benefit	
Sickness benefit	
Maintenance	
Retirement pension	
Other pensions	
Building society	
Post Office	
Bank deposit	
Contributions from members of household	
Any other	
Total	£

Analysing Chart Four – Income

The extent to which most people over-identify with their occupation (or lack of one) is surprising. For example, a company manager may turn down or be unaware of many extra income opportunities simply because he believes himself to *be* a manager. He is unable to see himself functioning in any other capacity. Other types of work may seem demeaning or poorly paid by comparison with his own comfortable niche; as a second income though, it could make all the difference between years of debt or a relatively quick recovery. Another example might be of a housewife who, having raised the children, slips into boredom and decline because she (mistakenly) believes that her value as a wife and mother is diminished by the children's independence. What about her own? There is nothing to prevent her from seeking full or part-time employment; nothing that is, except her own perception of herself as an 'employable' person. Indeed, today we see an unprecendented number of part-time vacancies intended for women, particularly in secretarial work and high technology. But there are many other possible jobs – bar staff, part-time market research and canvassing, sales work,home-working, self-employment, and so on.

Today, for better or worse, we no longer have the luxury of being able to identify, to the exclusion of all else, with any one work role. This is something which many of our European partners have recognised for a long time. It is not uncommon for them to take on two or even three jobs to provide the family income.

There is no reason why this should be an undesirable situation, provided the will exists to accept change in working practices and distribution of available employment. We are gradually witnessing a shift from people seeking employment in the traditional sense, towards people looking for ways to become self-employed.

One of the saddest features of the UK employment scene is that, over the years, a combination of restrictive working practice, weak management and unimaginative policies, have allowed industry to decline and collapse in the face of world competition. As a result, we have a pool of potential labour paid to be idle, not because they wish to be, but because industries with which they are traditionally associated no longer exist or have been run down to absolute minimum operating requirements. Over-identification with one working role for many years has led people to believe they are incapable of working in or are untrainable for any other occupation. This is both harmful and wasteful because such attitudes are limiting for the individual, and ultimately, a great loss to the nation. The fact is that there are a great many new jobs being created in new areas of work – services, arts, crafts, entertainment, social services, and so on. Why should a coalminer not learn to operate a computer? And why should a business executive not learn to be a tradesman? There is nothing to stop anybody from making fundamental changes in their working lives if they are convinced that is what they need to do. In the meantime, there are thousands of second income opportunities for those needing to supplement take-home pay. All you need is the will to do it. For example, there are thousands of business opportunities advertisements to be found in publications such as *Exchange & Mart* each week. Some may be non-starters, but many are worth closer investigation.

Unemployment and supplementary benefits

If, for the moment, this is your only source of income, you should ensure that you are receiving your full entitlement. Around 13 million people claim supplementary benefits of some description each year, but what is less well known is that about 25% of those eligible to claim do *not* do so. This is because they are either unaware of their rights or shy away from the beaurocracy involved in processing claims. There can be no doubt that the state benefit system intrudes deeply into personal matters, which understandably puts off a great many legitimate claimants. However, if you are in debt – or are about to be – you need every penny you can claim. The DHSS has published a leaflet entitled *Which Benefit* which is a guide to all the benefits currently available from the system, and is available from DHSS offices, post offices and Citizen's Advice Bureaux. You can also telephone Freefone DHSS and a copy will be sent to you free of charge.

This book cannot claim to specialise in the Social Security System, other than to advise you to claim the maximum to which you are entitled. An excellent book on the subject giving full details in layman's language is *The Penguin Guide to Supplementary Benefits*. Written by Tony Lynes, this is a mine of information which is otherwise largely unavailable to the general public.

If you have never claimed before, be warned. The procedure can be very depressing and sometimes humiliating. You must be prepared to accept a level of support barely above the official poverty line and hope to make ends meet. If you earn any money while claiming, all but the first £4 is taken into account and your benefit reduced accordingly. You will be asked to complete a multiplicity of forms and declarations of 'honesty' at regular intervals, including questions such as 'what attempts are you making to find suitable employment?', 'provide written details of all interviews attended and their outcome, with dates and times', and 'how far are you willing to travel to find work?'. Adjudication officers, who decide on your eligibility to benefit, are empowered to reduce your entitlement if they feel you are making insufficient efforts to seek work.

New legislation, part of which was introduced in August 1986, has begun to erode the number and type of benefits available, and also the numbers of people who may claim them. If this is your only means of support, do try to get off it as soon as possible – or harden yourself to the stark realities of Social Security.

Savings accounts

Nobody would deny the merit of having a nice little nest-egg tucked away, earning interest in a building society or bank deposit account. If you have debts though, the interest that you are charged very much outweighs anything you may earn from your savings. Depending on the size of your debts and savings, it might be a good idea to use some or all of them to clear your debts, and make a fresh start.

Use Chart Four as a basis for assessing your monthly or weekly income. Disregard any overtime unless it is a regular feature of your work. Do not include bonus or profit-share payments until you know they will be awarded, when and by how much. All your figures should take into account tax and National Insurance, where applicable.

Another way of increasing your income is to ask for a rise. Who knows, your talents may be worth more than you think, and you will not know until you approach your employer. You could also try some market research of your own by finding out what rival companies or organisations are paying for your kind of skills. You will of course, need to be discreet in your enquiries, but this kind of information can often tip the scales in pay negotiations. Your employer might even be willing to lend you money, although, you will probably have to tell him or her the reason for the loan, which may not leave him with the best impression of your management skills.

You may have children at home who, although working, pay far less than the going rate for board and lodging. Just think of the service which is probably provided for them; shelter, food, washing, television, telephone . . . all for a few pounds a week? No parent wants to seem mean, demanding exorbitant sums from their children, but they too, must learn what the real world is all about, and that includes paying one's way. As a general guide, you should charge 25% - 30% of take-home pay towards their share of the home.

If the children have left home and you have two or three rooms to spare, have you considered taking in lodgers? Many people shrink from the idea of having their homes invaded by total strangers, but it need not be that way. One agreeable and fairly lucrative method of letting out rooms is to attach yourself to agencies dealing with foreign students and business people.

You normally have to provide breakfast and an evening meal, but for between £45 - £60 a week, per person, is that really a great deal of trouble? More and more people are turning to this method of increasing income; the extra work is not hard, especially if you have been used to bringing up a family. The disadvantages are that you do lose a degree of privacy, though many students will be out for most of the time, at school or socialising while business people tend to use this kind of accommodation just for eating and sleeping. You will probably have to declare this income for tax purposes, but then you are allowed to offset any legitimate expenses incurred in the running of your business.

Analysing Chart Five – Assets

The list below gives examples of the kind of household items which could be sold if necessary.

Your home

Especially in the south of England, house prices in the UK have risen steadily, even spectacularly over the last few years. Your home may therefore be worth far more than you imagine, particularly if you bought it many years ago and have little or no mortgage to pay. Even if you are a first-time buyer and have lived in your home for only a year or two, the build up of equity is likely to be substantial. Selling the home though, is a stressful and time-consuming affair. You will need to buy a cheaper home, or rent. You will have to pay legal fees and removal expenses,so unless the benefits significantly outweigh the clear disadvantages, selling the home is not an attractive option.

The fact that you have a substantial asset in the property is more to your advantage than if you were to dispose of it; indeed it may be the only reason why creditors have not yet foreclosed, hoping that the value of your property increases until such time as there is enough equity to repay your debts. Most importantly, the home symbolises security and togetherness, the loss of which often leads to marital breakdown and a splitting of the family. Keep it, if you can.

Car

The sale of this one asset could make a big impact on your debts. You

Chart Five

ASSETS

Item	**Present value**
House/flat	
Car	
Hi-fi	
Video	
TV	
Boat	
Antiques	
Furniture	
Savings accounts	
Insurance policies	
Private pension fund	
Clothes	
Sports equipment	
Camera	
Jewellery	
Debts owed to you	
Tax rebate	
Bric-a-brac	
Another job	
Record collection	
Art collection	
Any others	
Total	£

will not necessarily have to go without a car either, if your current model is fairly new and in good condition. You could sell it, clear off any hire-purchase repayments outstanding and have enough left over to buy a smaller model for cash, or use the money to settle other debts. But if a car is essential to your livelihood, there are plenty to be had from amongst the second-hand or used car market. This is one very buoyant industry today as many people, often because of redundancy or unemployment, are forced to 'trade down' their cars for smaller, more economical models.

You could also consider selling your car for a 'run-about', pay back the finance company and use the balance to start your own little car business, buying and selling one or two a month to start with, gradually building up as time and funds allow. You may even be able to persuade your bank to assist in the project, if you can put forward a convincing argument.

Hi-fi/video/television

If you own these outright, you may be tempted to put an advert in the local paper or trade magazine, offering them for sale. Before you do, check the current second-hand prices being commanded for your type of equipment; you may be surprised, if not shocked at how little it is worth. The fact is, there is a price war taking place in the retail trade sector which has had, and will continue to have, a diminishing effect on second-hand values. Also, with all the 'easy' credit terms available for new equipment, your second-hand goods are immediately less attractive.

Run through the other items in this list and try to estimate their value. If you have insurance policies with savings attached, ring your broker and find out what the current 'cashed-in' value is. Also find out if you can borrow against the eventual cash value of the policy. The same goes for a private pension fund, if you have one.

Other assets which may be of some value are antiques left mouldering in the attic. Dust them off and have them valued at an auction room – not by the local antique dealer!

When you have completed Chart Five, add up the total, less realistic expenses you will incur in selling your assets. Is there enough to pay off your debts? With the house thrown in, it is likely that there will be, but we have already established that parting with the home is a last-ditch measure. What about the rest of your assets, how much of your debt will they cover, and is it worthwhile selling them? This decision is very personal and should not be made lightly, however, if you part with the bulk of your possessions, at least you will be free of the stress and worries of debt, and have the opportunity of rebuilding once again as and when you can afford it. This option is mentioned for one good reason: if your debts are £750 or more, your creditor(s) are empowered, under new legislation, to make you bankrupt very much more rapidly than hitherto. Almost any other course of action is preferable to that, as we shall discover, so do give serious thought to this advice, and do not let creditors or the courts get into a position of administering your affairs, if at all possible. There are only very few circumstances where this can be of benefit to the debtor (see chapter seven, arrears and court orders).

Now you are armed with all the information you need to compile your budget.This is a personal cash-flow chart, monitoring your expenditure month to month. The big advantage of this system is that we are going to use it to project your total outlay for periods of three months at a time. So, if you have done your homework, you will know, almost to the penny, what you are going to spend for the next 12 weeks. There will be no more nasty surprises because you are going to use this document in conjunction with your creditors. Your bank manager will see it, and anybody else financially relevant to you at present.

In business,the cash-flow statement is a vitally important tool in projecting the health of the business in the future. It is by this means that managers can predict sales, profits or losses, and generally steer as calm a course as possible. There need be no difference in your case. We have already mentioned the advantage of treating your affairs as a business, so let us now prepare the budget which, incidentally, is intended for both families and individuals.

How to fill in the debt-buster budget (see page 63)

If you find columns and rows of figures confusing, try not to be put off; the budget is really simple to complete and understand. It is, in fact, merely an extension of your analysing charts, but with a little more detail, and covering a period of three months. Working in three-monthly cycles is perhaps the simplest method for it is not too difficult to project that far ahead, once your finances have been restored to some kind of order.

To help you understand the chart and its significance, we have chosen a family with debt problems, James and Margaret Rushden. They have two children at school, and Margaret's sister Jennifer is staying with the family for the time being. Margaret is a registered childminder and James works as a middle manager in a large retail chain.

Section 'A' – Income

James' take-home pay is £700 per month. Margaret earns around £120 per month, in addition to child benefit of £56.80 per month. Jennifer contributes £80 a month to the household.

Sections 'B1', 'B2' and 'B3'

These correspond to the essential, important and periodic outgoings listed on your debt-analyser charts. Along the top of the chart, from left to right, are the headings Month one, two and three. Month one corresponds to the present month, and this should therefore be inserted. Under each month heading are three columns: budget amount, actual amount and balance.

Budget amount – month one

These are the figures taken from your debt-analyser charts, and represent your starting position. Simply work through sections 'A', 'B1', 'B2' and 'B3', slotting in the appropriate figures. If some of your income or expenses do not fall into any of the categories shown, allocate your own. To find your sum total of expenditure, add columns 'B1', 'B2' and 'B3'. James and Margaret have found out that they are currently spending £172.75 a month more than they earn, but, up until now,were never able to account for this.

Actual amount – month one

Repeat the exercise as above, this time using the actual amounts you earn and spend. In James' and Margaret's case, you can see from all the 'nils' against expenses such as water rates, gas, electricity, telephone, ground rent, car tax, insurance and maintenance, that they do not actually provide for any of these outgoings.

A quick glance at their credit card spending reveals that they are paying back £87.50 a month on these items. They actually owe £1,000 on one and £750 on the other, but can only afford to make minimum repayments (5% of the outstanding amount). They also have an unsecured bank loan for a car which they are paying back at £96.50 a month. Their total actual expenditure for month one is £944 – which is £22.20 more than they earned. But this is a false picture, since we know from their budget amount that they should be spending £172.75 more than their earnings! They also have a £300 overdraft at the bank

Debt-buster budget

	Month One			Month Two			Month Three		
	Budget	Actual	Balance	Budget	Actual	Balance	Budget	Actual	Balance
Income (A)									
Salary – Self	700.00	700.00		700.00	700.00		700.00	700.00	
Spouse	120.00	135.00		120.00	140.00		120.00	120.00	
Household	80.00	80.00		80.00	80.00		80.00	80.00	
Child benefit	56.80	56.80		56.80	56.80		56.80	56.80	
TOTAL (A)	956.80	971.80	971.80	956.80	976.80	976.80	956.80	956.80	956.80
Expenditure (B)									
Essential Outgoings (B1)	In each month the total balance from the previous month is added or subtracted here				Add +22.20 to			Subtract −54.83 from	
Mortgage	200.00	200.00		200.00	200.00		200.00	200.00	
Rates	50.00	50.00		50.00	50.00		50.00	50.00	
Water rates	8.00	NIL		8.00	8.00		8.00	8.00	
TV licence	4.80	NIL		4.80	4.80		4.80	4.80	
Electricity	42.00	NIL		42.00	37.00		37.00	37.00	
Gas	17.00	NIL		17.00	17.00		15.00	15.00	
Telephone	20.00	NIL		20.00	15.00		15.00	15.00	
TOTAL (B 1)	341.80	250.00	250.00	341.80	354.00	354.00	329.80	274.97	274.97
Important Outgoings (B2)									
Food &	200.00	225.00		200.00	185.00		185.00	185.00	
Housekeeping				44.91	44.91		96.50	81.50	
Bank loans	96.50	96.50		96.50	96.50		44.91	44.91	
Overdraft*	300.00	325.00		300.00	325.00		325.00	270.17	
Credit store cards 1	50.00	50.00		NIL	NIL		NIL	NIL	
2	37.50	37.50		NIL	NIL		NIL	NIL	
Insurance – home	12.50	12.50		12.50	12.50		12.50	12.50	
life	20.00	20.00		20.00	20.00		20.00	20.00	
Car – fuel	97.50	86.00		97.50	85.00		85.00	80.00	
oil	2.50	1.00		2.50	1.00		1.00	1.00	
School dinners	7.00	7.00		7.00	7.00		7.00	7.00	
Mail order catalogue	10.00	10.00		10.00	10.00		10.00	10.00	
Pet food	20.00	18.00		20.00	18.00		18.00	18.00	
Milk	20.00	18.00		20.00	18.00		18.00	18.00	
TOTAL (B 2)	573.50	581.50	581.50	530.91	497.91	497.91	497.91	477.91	477.91
Periodic outgoings (B3)									
Ground rent	5.41	NIL		5.41	5.41		5.41	5.41	
Car – tax & mot	9.29	NIL		9.29	9.33		9.33	9.33	
Insurance	10.83	NIL		10.83	10.83		10.83	10.83	
Garage bills	20.83	NIL		20.83	NIL		20.83	25.00	
TV/video rental	25.00	25.00		25.00	7.00		7.00	7.00	
Dental bills	2.50	NIL		2.50	NIL		2.50	2.50	
General repairs	8.33	NIL		8.33	8.33		8.33	8.33	
Book/record club	17.50	17.50		17.50	NIL				
Presents	29.16	20.00		29.16	4.16		4.16	4.16	
Alcohol/tobacco	39.58	45.00		39.58	NIL				
Personal spending	45.82	55.00		45.82	25.00		25.00	25.00	
TOTAL (B3)	214.25	162.50	162.50	214.25	70.06	70.06	93.39	97.56	97.56
TOTAL (B) (1 + 2 + 3)	1129.55	994.00	994.00	1086.96	921.97	921.97	921.10	850.44	850.44
A−B = over or underspend against budget.	+172.75	+22.20	+22.20	+130.16	−54.83	−54.83	−35.70	−106.36	−106.36

*NB Although the overdraft is shown, do not add it into monthly expenditure. This is because an overdraft is an arrangement between you and the bank and does not form part of regular income or expense. The purpose of the budget is to reduce it steadily month by month by spending less than budget.

(overdrafts should not be added into your total expenditure – see chart).

'Balance' column

This merely identifies and isolates, for all to see, the actual amounts earned and spent in the month. Addition and subtraction are easier if these figures can be readily identified.

Summary – month one

James and Margaret are in debt because they are not exercising tight enough control over their money. Up until now they have been paying fuel and other bills on demand, often using credit cards or overdraft facilities for this purpose. Their personal spending is a little too high for comfort, in relation to what they should put aside for essentials. If they continue along this path, they will soon encounter serious difficulties, as the deficit is growing by around £172 a month. The debt-buster budget has helped them to identify the problem, and it is now up to them to decide how they should rectify the problem.

Whatever your personal situation, the debt-buster can help you to resolve it. The decisions you make will be translated into savings on the chart, and month by month, if you stay with it, you should see improvements in your finances. It can take anything from three months to a year to order your affairs properly.

The bank reconciliation

All payments that you make by cheque will be recorded on your bank statements (save for the most recent). However, you should certainly keep your own record of all your cheques and cash-point withdrawals.

First, you will need to ensure that you get bank statements regularly every month, or fortnight, depending on how heavily you use your account. Then you simply match up the information with what's written on your cheque stubs. Make sure cheque numbers and amounts tally, and then cross them off in your cheque book, and on the statement by putting an 'X' against each transaction.

Use the bank statement to record all receipts and withdrawals in between receiving statements. As you become better at this, you should find that each new statement follows on from your own information on the old. Always check with the bank if there are 'mystery' payments on your account; they do make mistakes occasionally, but these need to be pointed out by you. You can even work out how much your overdraft is costing, and the price of each cheque and cash-card transaction as well, by finding out the interest you are being charged and the costs per transaction. This is a valuable exercise, enabling you to discover where your money goes.

Chapter Six

How to deal with creditors

Can you conjure up a mental image of a creditor? Indeed, have you ever seen one? People tend not to imagine creditors as people, but as impersonal, amorphous organisations housed in imposing buildings; their only function in life being to wait for you to get into arrears so they can send in a bailiff to repossess your goods. We think of creditors as we do the taxman; a necessary evil with whom we communicate little, preferably not at all. This is a great pity, as well as being a grave misunderstanding of the creditors' role in your financial recovery programme.

Understandably, many people feel humiliated and ashamed — not to mention frightened and confused at being suddenly unable to repay a debt. Their first reaction is to withdraw and try to sort out the mess by themselves. Sometimes this goes on for a long time, and the creditor becomes concerned that the debt might not be repaid, and so sends a letter, reminding you that your account is overdue. It is here that a great many people lose their nerve and run for cover. Burying one's head in the sand in the hope that a deafening silence will make the creditor and the debt go away, only leaves another part of the anatomy temptingly exposed!

It should always be remembered that creditors have rights. Ultimately, they can invoke the law to force a debtor to pay up, and, in certain circumstances, the most drastic remedy open to them is to threaten, and then carry out, bankruptcy proceedings.

From the creditors' point of view this is a costly, time-consuming affair which could have been avoided if you had communicated your difficulties to them in the first place. The buildings which house creditor organisations may well be grey and depressing, but they are populated with flesh and blood, real human beings. And they have their problems, including financial ones, just like everyone else. The clerk operating the computer terminal dealing with your account may have limited discretion if you fall into arrears. A prolonged silence leaves him no option but to press button 'A' – another threatening letter, only this time telling you that you may end up in court. The clerk after all, is only following company procedure. If, on the other hand, you tell the clerk your problem, he has to press button 'B' – refer to supervisor. Your case then becomes the subject of debate: what is the customer's track record? Has he defaulted before? How can we help this person, or is it too late to avoid proceedings? Or, 'yes, the proposals he has submitted seem reasonable, we will go along with them'.

Your creditors would much rather accept reduced payments over a longer period, voluntarily, than start legal proceedings against you, so forcing you to pay. As business people, they know that 50% of something is definitely better than 100% of nothing, which would probably be the position if you were bankrupted.

There are a few ground-rules which need to be observed when negotiating with creditors. If you put these into practice, it is a reasonable assumption that most, if not all of them, will help you out. Some may be more difficult than others, and results can never be guaranteed, but your attitude and persistence is paramount to the success of the operation.

You can get by with a little help from your friends . . . Rules for debtors

1. Do not panic.

2. If you have multiple debts, put them in order of priority – see debt analyser and debt-buster charts, page 63.

3. Always communicate in writing, keeping copies of all correspondence and notes of telephone conversations.

4. Be polite, honest and positive. Do not try to blame your creditor for what has happened to you (unless a series of errors on their part has caused the arrears; even then, be firm and business-like).

5. If you have multiple debts, tell each creditor, in writing, that you are informing all the others of your situation.

6. Always find out the name of the person and the department dealing with your account. Write to him or her personally, explaining your difficulties.

7. Always quote your account reference number in any correspondence.

8. If you get no result from the first letter, write another, this time to a superior, but be discreet. It is essential to maintain the goodwill of your creditor; and besides, no one likes to think they have been 'passed over'.

9. Some creditors take a tough line with debtors. Agree to initial demands, and then write again if you cannot meet them.

10. Do not give up, even if you think you have left it too late. Your creditor does not want to take you to court. Apart from the time and expense, the judge could well order in your favour, if you have been reasonable and tried to communicate with the creditor, making sensible repayment offers.

11. When making an offer of reduced payments, be realistic about the time you will need to pay back the debt. Give facts about figures, and estimates about time. If your creditor(s) agree to your proposal, and subsequently you find you cannot meet them, you should be able to re-negotiate, providing you have been reasonable from the start.

These 11 rules cover just about everything you will need to do in your attempts to win more time and / or reduce your payments.

Communication is so vital that it cannot be stressed forcefully and often enough. One of the major complaints made by creditor organisations is that customers in difficulty all too often keep quiet about their problems, fearing the worst from the creditor. The organisations stress, time and time again, the vital importance of continuing communication. That way your problems are shared, and can be dealt with in human terms, without the unpleasantness of threatening letters and legal action.

Whatever the reasons for your inability to repay, you owe it to your creditors to keep them properly informed of your circumstances if you expect them to help you. In chapter five, James and Margaret were in difficulties because they had overstretched their finances through not grasping the importance of making provision for essential and regular expenditure. This is a widespread problem, not caused by a wilful desire to get into difficulties, but because people do not know how to avoid them. Even if you have been downright foolish with your money, by admitting to it now you stand a better chance of gaining your creditors' respect. They may not like hearing what you have to say, but they will be more willing to help if they know you have been completely honest with them.

Letters to creditors

Irrespective of education and upbringing, a great many people seem unable to compose letters which convey a real sense of purpose or urgency when it comes to 'selling' themselves. In this case, you are selling the 'idea' that you are concerned about your affairs, and that you acknowledge the extent of the problem, but are willing and able to resolve it, given a little good will. Letter 'A' is an example which should elicit a sympathetic response. If you do not know the name of the person to whom you are writing, telephone the switchboard of the organisation concerned and ask the receptionist. At the same time, ask for the names of assistants and superiors, and also their telephone extension numbers. Since managers' schedules are often full it will sometimes be necessary to deal with an assistant. Do not let this put you off.

Letter 'A' to Building Society/Bank Manager

Mr V E Prudent,	25 Acacia Avenue,
Manager,	Midtown,
Barcloyds Bank Plc,	Surrey PX3 4HA.
Midwest Street	
Surrey TSB IUP	8th April 1987

Dear Mr Prudent,

Account No / Mortgage Agreement No: 62534 / BLAH / 2468

I am writing to advise you that, having recently lost my job / been made redundant, I will not / have not been able to meet my normal monthly payment on the above account.

I am taking every step in seeking suitable alternative employment and hope to be able to resume normal payments as soon as possible. In the meantime, you will appreciate that I am very concerned about this matter, and would welcome the opportunity of discussing some form of agreement with the Bank / Building Society.

I will telephone your secretary within the next few days to arrange an appointment, so that I can discuss the matter with you.

Yours sincerely,

John Badlioff

This letter will probably receive the following response:

Dear Mr Badlioff,

Thank you for your letter dated 8th April 1987. I am sorry to hear of your present difficulties, and would be pleased to make arrangements to see you.

Please telephone my secretary, Mr Orderly, to make an appointment.

Yours sincerely

V E Prudent, Manager

It would be very difficult indeed to imagine a response which is less than sympathetic to your letter, provided you have no previous record of arrears.

Letter 'B' would be more suited to credit card and finance companies, particularly where the administration offices are some distance from your home. In these circumstances, a meeting is nearly always out of the question and your letter must speak for you.

Letter 'B' to credit card or finance company

Mrs F G Friend,
Accounts Manager,
Ucanhavitt Finance Co Ltd,
Scunthorpe 9XX.

25 Acacia Avenue,
Midtown,
Surrey PX3 4HA.
10th April 1987

Dear Mrs Friend

Re: Account No. 123476/0987

I am writing to inform you that, having recently lost my job/been made redundant, I am temporarily unable to meet the normal monthly payments on the above account. For the present, the amount I can afford is £ , , and I therefore enclose a cheque herewith trusting that you find this acceptable.

In the meantime, I am taking all possible steps to secure new employment, and will of course keep you advised of progress.

Yours sincerely,

John Badlioff

PS I have written similar letters to all my creditors, who so far have kindly expressed a willingness to help.

Letters to those who can help you

Do you recall that much-advertised slogan of the electricity companies, 'We have the power to help you'? Now is the time to test that promise. In fact, if you are in difficulties with your fuel and telephone bills, then all your service creditors should get a letter, offering to pay the present accounts over a period of say, three months, so they are settled in time for the next bill. You should also ask about budget account facilities, using direct debit through your bank. You can also buy stamps from the post office towards the cost of your next television licence and telephone bill. If your finances really are bleak, you may have to think about going without a telephone and / or television for a while. This should not be necessary however, if your creditors rally round.

The gas, electricity and telephone companies are 'high profile' organisations, that is, they continually advertise on television and in the newspapers. The kind of images they like to project vary, ranging from mild paternalism to trite affability. But they all have one thing in common, and that is the need for good publicity. They do not want to lose your custom, no matter how severe your problems may seem. They also nurture reputations of integrity and customer service, so in your attempts to reach a compromise, you can capitalise on this.

Letter 'C' should help provoke the desired response.

Letter 'C' to gas / electricity / telephone

25 Acacia Avenue
Midtown
Surrey PX3 4HA

Ms E Sparks
Customer Accounts Manager
Customer Accounts Department
Gas / Electricity / Telephone Co
Central Street
Surrey PX1 7EW

12th April 1987

Dear Ms Sparks

Re: Account No: 658495 / 8723645

I am writing to inform you that, having been made unemployed / redundant (whatever the reason), I find I am unable to pay the full amount of the above account at the moment. I realise this is very inconvenient for you, but am enclosing a cheque for one third of the amount and plan to send two further cheques for the same sum, over the next two months.

I am sure that you will appreciate the difficulty of my present circumstances and would not wish my family to suffer hardship. I shall be happy to settle accounts in the normal way as soon as matters have returned to normal.

In the meantime, would you kindly send me details of your budget account facilities for the future.

Thanking you for your kind assistance.

Yours sincerely

John Badlioff

PS. I have contacted my other creditors in the same way, and so far, all have kindly agreed to help.

Example 3: How to work out what to pay to whom

James and Margaret Rushden earn enough to pay all their debts, if they put their house in order. We shall see at the end of this chapter how they got on with their creditors and what their completed personal budget sheet looks like for the first three months. Your situation may be somewhat different, in that you do not actually earn enough to cover all your outgoings. Providing your creditors agree, the following calculations should serve as a guide to what to offer them.

Example 4: Paying the essential bills; compromising on the others

Suppose your net income is £9,000 a year.

Your essential outgoings are	£4,000	A
Important outgoings	£5,000	B
Periodic outgoings	£2,000	C
Total	£11,000	

So, from your net income of £9,000, subtract your essential outgoings (A) £4,000. This leaves £5,000, to pay the important (B) and periodic (C) outgoings which amount to £7,000. To find out what percentage of the two categories can be paid from the remaining £5,000 you divide £5,000 by £7,000 (B + C) which gives you an answer of 0.714. If you multiply this figure by 100% you can determine the percentage of each bill or expense which can be paid from the £5,000. In this case the figure is 71.40%. In practice though, it may not be so easy. Can you cut back your food and housekeeping by 30%, or reduce the children's clothes by 30%? Clearly, there will be instances where the formula cannot apply, but if you can secure some concessions from your creditors, the burden will be measurably eased.

If the foregoing measures are still not enough to restore your finances, you must write to your creditors, asking them to waive payments for a few months. This will work only with creditors such as the bank, building society and possibly finance house, rates authority and credit card company. It is, unfortunately, unlikely to work with gas, electricity and telephone bills: these authorities are more likely to disconnect you and prosecute for any arrears.

Month two — stabilising measures

To return to James and Margaret, who as we saw spent £22.20 more than they earned last month. This has to be accounted for somewhere in the personal budget. We have decided to allocate the deficit (and any future savings!) at the top of column 'B1' – essential outgoings: and to put a plus (+) sign in front of the amount. This immediately tells us they must add the £22.20 to their total expenditure for the month, before anything else. Likewise, if they underspend or make any savings against their budgeted expenditure for a full month, they should carry this amount over to the next month, again putting the figure at the top of column 'B1' but this time with a minus (−) sign in front of it. This means they should subtract this amount from their expenditure for the month. Gradually the 'minuses' or underspends will increase month by month until their affairs are back in order. It is essential to record the pluses and minuses at the top of column 'B1' because this is the starting point for all their outgoings. So, if they overspend one month, it means they have less to start with for the next and vice versa.

Next, they contacted the gas, elecricity and telephone companies, requesting application forms to pay by direct debit in future. They also resolved to cut fuel consumption by at least £5 per month in the short term.

Margaret believed she could pare the food and housekeeping budget down by £15 per month, and set this as her target.

Then they opened a building society account especially for all the periodic outgoings such as car tax, insurance, garage bills, television licence and so on. From their debt analysis charts, they decided to save amounts equivalent to their average monthly expenditure on these items (they would also earn interest on the deposits as well).

They were worried that they had let their credit card spending get out of hand. Paying back the minimum amount each month made virtually no inroad to the debt, and so James went to see the bank manager, to try to negotiate a 'consolidation loan' to clear in one bite the debt with the credit card companies.

The manager agreed to this, providing that they also made some headway with their overdraft, which had now crept up to £325. James showed the manager his personal budget, which forecast they would actually be in credit at the month end, and would soon be able to pay the overdraft off. They took out an unsecured loan for £1,750 over five years, at an annual percentage rate of 19.8%, giving monthly repayments of £44.91 – so saving around £42.59 a month on credit card payments – plus a great deal of potential interest as the equivalent annual percentage rate on these is around 27% at the time of writing.

James used the car for work, and decided to save fuel by leaving a little earlier in the mornings to beat the rush hour, which did indeed improve his miles-per-gallon consumption.

When it came to savings on periodic outgoings, they had some soul-searching to do. They realised that they could sell the car and save on all the running costs and insurance, but felt that this would not be fair on the rest of the family. They reserved this option as a last resort. Instead, they decided to return their underused video to the rental company, saving £18 a month, and also cut down on drinking and smoking for a few months at least.

All in all, they had created a fairly radical recovery programme which, by the end of the month, would put their finances £38.83 in the black. They certainly considered this a worthwhile move, especially as month three would show an even greater improvement.

Another important decision which James and Margaret made was not to use their credit cards for a while, realising that these had been a big drain on their money. When everything else was under control, they would work out a different system of using them which would make a positive rather than a negative contribution to their cash flow.

They were also horrified to learn they had spent about £300 on Christmas presents last year and decided that would not happen again. If they managed to stabilise their finances during the next six months, they would then review the decision next December.

Month three — the finishing touch

Since their efforts were now beginning to pay dividends, James and Margaret began to think about ways of increasing their income. Margaret's student sister, Jennifer, was staying with the family for the duration of her course. Margaret felt bound to help her financially, and therefore only took £80 per month for food. They discussed the situation with Jennifer who agreed that during holiday periods she would look for work and pay more towards her upkeep. Margaret worked from home as a childminder, but could take only one child in as her other two were still under school age. She worked overtime occasionally, when the mother of the little girl she looked after went late-night shopping or was delayed at the office. Margaret decided that she would seek alternative employment when the children were of school age — that way, her contribution would be even greater.

James was in line for promotion at the end of the year and therefore decided to make extra efforts at work, to secure his prospects, and pay rise. To ease their finances still further, James went to see his bank manager again, asking for a loan to 'repay' their car loan, which had been running for over 12 months. The manager agreed to this proposal, granting him a new loan costing £81.50 per month instead; a saving of £15.00 per month.

Their personal budget now showed a downward trend in their outgoings, with the budget and actual amounts following each other very closely. They were also managing to save such substantial amounts each month in the building society account that, by the end of the month, there was a credit balance of £106.36 in the bank account (which, naturally, went towards paying off their overdraft).

All they need to ensure now is that they continue to plan their finances as they have done for the past three months. They know that the loan outstanding for the car will be paid off in the next three years, so after that they will have an extra £81.50 in their pockets per month. Using the budget sheet, they can forecast their income and expenses month by month, for example, planning for a holiday next year. Christmas need no longer come as a nasty necessity, since they will agree on a set amount to put aside for presents. Of course, there will be occasional unforseen expenses, but as long as they are careful, it should not topple their budget balance. They will always have savings in the building society, which, although meant for essential and periodic outgoings, can be used in an emergency. If they go 'over budget' one month, they should try to cut back by the same amount during the next. Most importantly, they will be the masters of credit, and not its slave!

James and Margaret are probably typical of many thousands of families. The real point is that, whatever your situation, the personal budget will work for you if you let it. Nobody can deny that it calls upon us to review, and change if necessary, some aspects of our behaviour; and, sometimes, the situation may even have to get worse before it can get better. Sacrifices will have to be made, but these are nothing compared to the consequences of not dealing with the situation as soon as possible.

Completed budget sheets

Chart One James & Margaret Rushden April 1987

Essential Monthly Outgoings

Item	**Amount £**	**When due**	**Amount outstanding £**
Mortgage and Insurances	200.00	30th	27,000
Rent			
Mortgage/Rent arrears			
Second Mortgage			
Second Mortgage arrears			
Rates	50.00	6th	350.00
Rate arrears			
Water Rates	8.00	15th	88.00
Water Rate arrears			
TV Licence	4.80	Paid until June '87	Nil
Electricity	42.00		Nil
Gas	17.00		
Telephone	20.00		
Maintenance payments			
Court fines			
Total	341.80		27,438

Chart Two James & Margaret Rushden April 1987

Important Monthly Outgoings

Item		**Amount £**	**When due**	**Amount outstanding £**
Food and Housekeeping		200.00	Use cash/ credit cards	
Bank loans (unsecured)	1	96.50	7th	2316.00
	2			
	3			
Overdraft (unsecured)		300.00	Soon as poss.	300.00
Hire Purchase				
Credit cards	1	50.00	11th	1000.00
	2	37.50	26th	750.00
	3			
Home Insurance		12.50	Renewable August '87	
Life Insurance		20.00	Bankers Order 1st	
Pension Plan				
Telephone		See Essential Outgoings!		
Car: Fuel & Oil		100.00		
School Dinners		7.00		
Fares to work				
Mail order (list each one)		10.00		280.00
Pet food (dog & cat)		20.00		
Milk		20.00		
Total		573.50		4646.00

Chart Three James & Margaret Rushden April 1987

Other Periodic Outgoings Yearly Estimates

Item	**Amount £**	**When due**
Ground rent	65.00	November '87
Car: Tax	100.00	August '87
Insurance	130.00	August '87
MOT	11.50	August '87
Garage bills	250.00	Due for service soon!
TV rental Video rental	300.00	25.00 on 16th of month
Clothing	Usually buy through mail order / credit card	
Dental bills	30.00	Check up soon!
Opticians bills		
General repairs	100.00	
Book club	60.00	5.00 on 15th of Month
Record club	150.00	12.50 on 27th of Month
Christmas presents	300.00	
Birthday presents	50.00	
Alcohol	300.00	
Tobacco	175.00	
Subscriptions	50.00	Includes delivery of papers
School fees		
Sundry items	500.00	Personal spending James & Margaret
Total	2571.50	
Divide by 12 to give monthly average	214.25	

Chart Four James & Margaret Rushden

Income per month

Item	**Amount £**
Wages / Salary (not including occasional overtime)	
Man – salary	700.00 (net)
Woman – childminding	120.00
Child benefit	56.80
Unemployment benefit	
Supplementary benefit	
Invalidity benefit	
Sickness benefit	
Maintenance	
Retirement pension	
Other pensions	
Building society	
Post Office	
Bank deposit	
Contributions from members of household	80.00
Any other	
Total	956.80

Chart Five

Item	**Assets** **Present value**
House / Flat	36,000 (less purchase price 28,000)
Car	1,950 (about)
Hi-Fi	350
Video	Rented
TV	Rented
Antiques	200
Furniture	1,000
Savings Accounts	150
Insurance policies	300
Private pension fund	
Clothes	500
Sports equipment	100
Camera	150
Jewellery	1,000
Tax rebate	
Bric-a-brac	100
Another job	Thinking about it
Record collection	200
Art collection – few prints	100
Any others – stamp collection	200
Total	14,300

Chapter Seven

Arrears – how to deal with them, and creditors' rights

Mortgage arrears

If you miss a payment on your mortgage account, the mortgagee (lender) will send you a letter detailing the arrears, along with a polite request for the debt to be cleared and normal payments to be resumed. If you miss two or three payments the mortgagee, via their solicitors, will probably inform you that they intend to seek a possession order through the courts. In the meantime, the building society or bank will probably have tried to communicate with you by letter, by telephone, and sometimes even by tele-message. If you do not respond to that communication by contacting the lender, in writing, giving reasonable grounds for the default, then it is inevitable that you will be taken to court.

Repossession can take place only under a county court order, which means that you will receive a summons to appear at a specified date and time, issued by the mortgagee, through its solicitors. The hearing normally takes place within six to eight weeks of the summons being served, and will be before the registrar in chambers. It is vital that you attend the hearing if you are to stand any chance of keeping your home. The mortgagee and/or his representatives will be there with proof of the debt; you will have been notified of this fact not less than five days before the hearing. The court will sometimes accept oral evidence of the debt.

Although you will be fully aware of the reasons for the court hearing, do not assume that all is lost. If you can persuade the court that, through circumstances beyond your control (such as separation, divorce, unemployment or illness), there are compelling reasons why you should not lose the home, the registrar is empowered to make a suspended order for possession, subject to your meeting certain conditions. Normally, these will include a resumption of the repayments plus a monthly contribution towards the arrears. In cases of genuine hardship, the court is likely to be quite generous in fixing this contribution. On the other hand, if you have shown disregard for the creditor(s) or tried to deceive them, this will not impress the registrar, who will then probably order the arrears to be cleared fairly rapidly.

Contrary to popular opinion, the courts, aware of the many hardships confronting people today, tend to be generous with the time allowed to clear arrears — even though the mortgagee has brought proceedings. But if you default in future, the mortgagee is entitled to seek a warrant for possession without reference to you. It is therefore imperative that you communicate any difficulties with payments to the mortgagee, who may be prepared to accept even lower payments for a time. If the lender is unwilling to reconsider his position, you can apply to the court to have the payments varied. The court will send details of the application to the lender along with a date for a new hearing, when it will decide whether to amend its previous order. Clearly, if there is no reasonable prospect of the arrears and normal repayments being met, the court will have no alternative but to grant a warrant for possession.

Again, we come back to the golden rule, which is to communicate. Always remember that your creditors have rights — something often ignored in the argument — and that you owe it to them to keep them properly informed throughout your difficulties. In return, you can expect them to be reasonable with you. Noboby wants you to lose your home.

Being sued for debt

In chapter six we discussed the procedure for dealing with creditors and the necessity of keeping them fully informed of your circumstances. If you have not, or the creditor was unable to accept the proposals you made, he is entitled to sue you for the recovery of the debt.

The county court system

The county court system is the means for dealing with debts and other claims of up to £5,000. The county court jurisdiction also covers land — the possession of property either mortgaged or rented — the rateable value being the criterion as to whether the court has jurisdiction. Such jurisdiction applies when the rateable value does not exceed £1,000. In practice, this covers most types of property.

County court summons

This is a standard form which can be obtained from any county court office. The creditor, normally, through his solicitors, issues the summons to you, as debtor. You must communicate with the court within 14 days, otherwise judgement can be signed against you without any further notice from the creditor. There are two ways of filling in the form, according to whether you intend to admit or defend the claim.

Defended claim

If you intend to defend all or part of the claim, you must return the summons within 14 days, setting out the reasons for your defence in the space provided. The court will then notify the creditor and set a date for both parties to attend a pre-trial hearing.

Pre-trial review

This is not a proper hearing, but an informal meeting between the registrar and both parties. The purpose of the meeting is to allow both sides to bring forward any evidence, witnesses, and so on, and to establish a time-table for bringing the matter to trial. Often, the case can be resolved at this stage, without the necessity of a hearing. If so, the registrar 'rubber stamps' the agreement between the parties, which is binding.

Debtor admits claim

If there is no defence to the claim and you admit to the debt(s), you must complete the summons accordingly and return it within 14 days; either paying the debt in full, plus any costs endorsed on the summons, or, making an offer revealing how you will pay it. There is space on the form for you to set out your income, expenditure and offer. A copy of the summons will be sent to the creditor or his solicitors, and the creditor then has to decide whether to accept the offer or ask the court to adjudicate on the fairness of the offer. If the creditor does accept the offer, he must notify the court, who will inform you and advise when payments should begin (usually one month later). If the creditor refuses the offer, he must still notify the court who will set a date for a hearing which both parties must attend.

Since the court will decide whether you are telling the truth about your means, you should take evidence of all expenditure — bills, rent book, mortgage certificate, rates book, bank statements and so on. Based on this information, the court will decide whether the offer is fair, or set a level of payments itself. Both parties are bound by the decision of the court, but as we saw with mortgage arrears, if your situation worsens you must tell the creditor and the court, who may temporarily reduce the payments. Notice of county court judgements is released to credit reference agencies for use when lending organisations make routine credit enquiries.

Debts under £500 – 'the small claims court'

Where the debt is under £500 the registrar will hear the case in what is known as 'the small claims court', which is a form of arbitration where there is no appeal. The matter is dealt with informally, without formal rules of evidence, with the intention of discouraging the attendance of solicitors. No costs can be awarded, apart from the actual expenses for those people attending.

High court writ

This is normally served through the post, although it can be handed to you. It is accompanied by a form called a form of Acknowledgement of Service. This must be returned to the court within 14 days, with a declaration from you that either you admit the claim or want the opportunity of putting forward an offer. You are not required to set out your means or, if it is a defended claim, set out the defence.

There is a timetable of events involved in high court proceedings, and these must be strictly adhered to, otherwise the creditor, without further notice, can ask for a judgement to be signed against you. You can ask for the judgement to be set aside, but the burden of proof lies with you to give sound reasons as to why you did not comply with the terms of the writ or timetable of events. High court proceedings are usually the forerunner to bankruptcy (where the debt is over £5,000), and anybody in this position should seek legal advice *immediately*.

Administration order

Where the total debts do not exceed £5,000 the debtor can apply to the county court for an administration order to be made. This means that the court handles the debtor's financial affairs. The court writes to each creditor to inform them that you have asked for your affairs to be administered by the court, and asking whether they are willing for this to happen. A creditor does not have to agree to the proposal, but in practice, if it is the only chance he has of being paid, is likely to agree to such proposals. Under the administration order, the court decides who gets what from the remainder of your income. If the amount is low, the creditors will have to be prepared to accept drastically reduced payments over a long period of time. An administration order can only be granted at the debtor's request.

Attachment of earnings order

This often accompanies an administration order, and is a notice requesting your employer to deduct sums of money from your wage at regular, specified intervals, and send the payments to the court. The court then disburses the money amongst the creditors. The system is flawed though, for if you are unemployed or change jobs frequently, the order is virtually unenforceable.

Rent arrears

At the time of writing, one London local authority has reported £23 million in rent arrears alone. The total for London is £125 million. Add to this every other local authority and private landlord unable to collect rents and the problem becomes massive, affecting literally millions of people. It is very easy to fall behind with the rent, especially when other payments seem more pressing, and you do not own the home anyway. The consequences for tenants, however, are the same as for so-called home owners. If you fall far enough behind with your rent, your council or landlord will eventually serve a notice to quit which, if not complied with, will be followed by an eviction order. You may then be evicted, forcibly if necessary.

Private tenants

The vast majority of private landlords, with the exception of housing associations, are not in the property business through love of it or a sense of social duty. They are in it for the money. With increasing purchase prices combined with a very serious cutback in public housing, the demand for housing of all types far outstrips supply. This is an ideal situation for profiteering on the part of landlords. If you feel your rent is too high, you should apply to the rent officer to come and inspect your property. He may order a fair rent to be set which could be a good deal lower. He also has the power to increase rents too, if he feels they are too low.

If you are in arrears with your rent, your landlord is less likely to be as sympathetic towards your plight as a local authority, for example. It may be his only source of income, so unless you are in a position to assure him that you will soon be able to make up the arrears while continuing to pay your normal rent, you may find yourself with a notice to quit. Again, the golden rule is communication. Talk to the landlord; write to him. Do anything to persuade him that you are seriously trying to overcome your present difficulties. If you try to avoid him by being 'out' whenever he calls, you are only bringing the day of the eviction order closer. Incidentally, you should always register your name on the local authority housing list when in private rented accommodation. You may not qualify for a council home at the moment, but your circumstances may change, for example, through marriage and/or having children, which will increase your points rating with the council.

In the event of your being served with a notice to quit, there are certain procedures to follow. First, contact your landlord to see if you can still reach an agreement. If you are withholding rent because he has failed to provide some basic service, contact your local Citizen's Advice Bureau and/or Housing Aid Centre, who will be able to advise you about your rights as a tenant. However, if no agreement is reached, you will receive a court summons. Accompanying the summons is a form of admission or defence. You should complete and return this.

If your case is complicated because you are counterclaiming, you should seek legal advice and you may be entitled to legal aid. Contact the Citizen's Advice Bureau who will advise you on this matter. Nobody relishes the prospect of going to court, but you must attend otherwise the registrar will assume that you admit to the facts laid out and grant an eviction order. By attending court you have an excellent opportunity to present your case with or without legal representation. The registrar is most likely to make a suspended order, meaning that you can remain in the home for as long as you pay your normal rent plus a contribution towards arrears, an amount which will be fixed by the court. Make sure that you or your representative present the full facts about your financial circumstances. If the registrar is convinced that there is genuine hardship he will be more likely to decide in your favour. In any event, judges and registrars are very loath to evict people unless they have to. If you still cannot afford to keep up payments after a suspended order has been made, then you should speak to your landlord again. He may agree to a reduced offer rather than going to the bother of taking out court proceedings again. But even if your landlord does take you back to court, providing you can demonstrate that you have maintained the agreed payment up until now, the registrar may order a lower payment in your favour. But if you have allowed arrears to build up again, he will have no choice but to grant the eviction order and you will be homeless before long.

Council tenants

If you live in a council home and are in arrears with your rent, then the same principles apply as if you were a private tenant. However, because so many council tenants are in arrears, many councils have adopted a sympathetic policy towards tenants in genuine financial hardship. Councils are forced into this position by the dire lack of alternative housing available elsewhere. Since housing is a key political issue today no council wants to gain the reputation of being a ruthless 'evictor'. Your housing officer, estate manager or rent collector is the person you should contact if you fall into arrears. If only moderate sums are involved you will be allowed to make your normal payment, plus a small contribution towards the arrears every week. If, for some reason, your financial circumstances have changed permanently, due, for example, to the family leaving home, illness or redundancy, you should consider a transfer to a smaller, more manageable property. The council have their own list of transfers available and you can look in local newspapers and corner shop windows to see if other tenants are looking for a property like yours.

If your arrears involve large sums of money the council may be prepared to write off part or all of the debt if there is no hope of recovery, provided that you continue to make normal payments. If you are threatened with a notice to quit from the local authority you have the right to take up the matter with your MP and local councillor. In genuine cases, these people will be pleased to pursue your case and do everything possible to keep you in your home. Do not be daunted because they are public figures. They are there to serve the needs and protect the rights of their constituents, regardless of political persuasion or status.

Being evicted through rent arrears will not necessarily entitle you to be re-housed by the council. They may regard your non-payment as an act of making yourself 'intentionally homeless' and are not forced to meet their statutory obligation to provide you with a home. Also, it might prove very difficult to find rented accommodation elsewhere since landlords almost invariably require references, and they will be reluctant to take on someone with a history of non-payment.

Rate arrears

The General Rate (a tax on property ownership) is levied by central government and collected by your local authority. Unless you live on a barge or in a caravan there is no escape from paying rates, and the punishment for non-payment is a heavy fine and / or imprisonment. It is therefore a criminal offence to evade payment, which is dealt with in a magistrates court. This is not at all like a civil court. If you disobey a summons to appear, you face the possibility of bailiffs calling to seize goods from your home to settle the debt. Items for which you may have saved for years to buy, will be seized and sold for next to nothing. So, if you are unable to meet your rate demand you should contact the finance department of your local council immediately, in writing, stating your circumstances. You will normally be given an opportunity to settle the demand by whatever means available before the next year's rate demand is out. If you are on a low income or are unemployed, make sure that you are claiming any housing benefit and rate allowance to which you may be entitled. Your local DHSS will advise you whether you are entitled to claim benefit on completion of a questionnaire. Many people feel degraded at having to go through this declaration of means. However, this is the time to swallow your pride and get any benefits and help to which you are entitled.

The knock on the door — bailiffs

If you are in the unfortunate position of having to open your door to a bailiff there are certain goods that he cannot remove. Anything not owned by you personally or goods which are the subject of a hire-purchase agreement which are the legal property of the finance company, cannot be taken. If you have documentary evidence or proof of other people's ownership of goods in your household, you should show it to the bailiff. The bailiff cannot remove essential clothing or the tools of your trade up to the value of £250 (in 1986).

A bailiff is a court official who must have proof of identity and a copy of the court order against you. Before allowing him to enter your home you should check these details carefully. Bailiffs have wide ranging powers of entry onto premises, although they are not permitted to seize goods on Sundays. If, however, you refuse them entry from Monday to Friday, day or night, they are empowered to use reasonable force to gain entry. You can also be committed for contempt of court if you resist the bailiff in discharging his duties. The court can then empower him to enter your home at any time, using whatever force is necessary. All of this is extremely unpleasant and humiliating. Obviously you need to take whatever legal advice you can if you suspect that bailiffs are going to be knocking at your door. If your goods, when sold, do not fetch enough to repay your debts in full, your creditors can petition for your bankruptcy, even though it will cost them money to do so.

Distress warrant

A distress warrant is also known as a warrant of execution against goods. This empowers a bailiff to enter your home between sunrise and sunset for rent arrears (any reasonable time for other debts), except Sundays. He can seize your goods to sell them at an auction in order to pay the debt. A bailiff cannot use force to enter a flat or house, although he can enter an open window or skylight. He can then break down any inside door to gain access to your property. If the warrant is for rent arrears he can take property which belongs to other people. He may not do so for rates arrears. If he does remove property belonging to other people or a finance company, it is then the duty of the rate-payer to inform them so they can claim the goods back from the bailiff. If the goods have already been sold off then the rate-payer is liable to the owner for their value. If the bailiff takes something that does not belong to you, but in good faith, you cannot sue afterwards.

This is a warning. Although the prospect of court attendances may seem daunting, you should always attend and put your case forward, otherwise the court will order in favour of the creditor without further notice. Proceedings at county court level are informal compared with those in the high court, and so no one need fear them. Of course, it is better not to get to this stage at all, and that is why we come back to communication. A great many people who now have judgements for debt against them, could have avoided this situation had they only conducted their affairs in a proper manner, by talking to the creditors. Even if one or two creditors are reluctant to agree to offers, you can use this as evidence in court and will probably win the day — certainly if other creditors have agreed to these instalments, and providing your offer was reasonable.

Legislation introduced on December 29, 1986 has now made the ordeal of bankruptcy even more strenuous. It is far better to do your utmost to come to an amicable settlement, even if it means appearing before a registrar or judge, than to let the situation deteriorate unchecked.

Chapter Eight

Types of personal finance

During the past decade Britain has engaged in more and more money lending, with banks, finance houses, foreign investors and building societies pumping hundreds of billions of pounds into the economy. And in the face of general industrial decline and high interest rates, the British public has become a lucrative and willing source of profit for the lending organisations. Indeed, an entire consumer boom is being financed by credit, for as we saw earlier credit (or debt) in the first part of 1986 accounted for some 72% of disposable income.

How your creditworthiness is assessed

In the past, if you wanted a loan from the bank, you used to have to make an appointment to see the manager. During the course of the interview, he would find out certain things about you: where you lived, how much you earned and your 'prospects'. He would also weigh you up by the way you dressed and your general demeanour. This could be unfortunate if you were not particularly good at presenting a viable proposition, or if your image did not tally with his notion of a reliable customer. Bank managers had a great deal more power in those days, and television commercials depicted them virtually as an extension of the home, residing in people's wardrobes, appearing at just the right moment. This kind of approach has now almost entirely given way to new methods of credit assessment. These days you no longer even have to know the name of your bank manager to be able to borrow – technology and statistical analysis take care of the whole process.

When you complete a loan application form, a hire-purchase or credit sale agreement, you have to declare certain facts about your present financial and personal circumstances. The lender, although relying to a great extent on your honesty, normally has the information processed through a computer, at the offices of one of the two major credit information agencies in the country. These agencies process and record millions of enquiries each year, and the kind of information they provide to the lender is whether you have any county court judgements for debt against you, you are a bankrupt (or have been), and there are records of previous arrears, default or refusals to grant credit. If you get the all-clear from the agency, the lender then has to decide whether to make an advance. That decision will be based entirely on the commercial probability that you will repay, given your information and the lender's past experience of lending to people in similar circumstances. But how does the lender arrive at a sound commercial judgement?

Credit scoring

This system is hailed by many as the fairest and most reliable method of assessing the likelihood of a person repaying a loan. Although few will have heard of it, credit scoring has been in existence for around 40 years, and the statistical techniques which it employs have been routinely improved and updated during this time, particularly since the Consumer Credit Act of 1974. Credit scoring measures the probability that credit will be repaid by predicting the performance of given groups with the same characteristics, based on the past performance of groups with the same characteristics.

It is claimed that credit scoring removes the subjectivity from decision making, and enables a lender to organise his affairs better, and to provide a better customer service. In addition to the usual range of questions about place of residence, job and how long you have been employed, credit scoring enquires into your 'status' as a person. Do you have a profession? Are you skilled / semi or unskilled / a housewife / unemployed / a member of the armed forces; and so on. Questions are asked about your financial commitments, your mortgage, other debts, net household income after expenses, and so on. Each category of answer bears certain points or 'weightings' so if, for example, you are a householder, have a secure job and steady income, you will get a 'good' score and the lender is likely to make an advance. The system is not infallible, however. If you have just moved house, got a new job (perhaps with better pay), or have become self-employed, your score would probably be marked down simply because in your new position you have no track record. In these circumstances, you may be refused a loan under the credit scoring system, whereas an interview with a bank manager might well have secured you a loan.

In striving to be completely objective, credit scoring misses one vital element — the human one. It works in set ways and can only approve certain categories. It cannot tackle the unusual. Whereas such deals were once conducted on trust, and on acceptance of the customer's word, this is no longer always the case.

It is clear that the accuracy of credit scoring will become increasingly wayward as more and more people make use of credit as a primary source of finance. There are going to be many more potential 'bad debtors' through unemployment, divorce and taking on multiple debts, than in the past.

Assuming that you have now been cleared as a reliable borrower, what kinds of loans are available to you?

Loans

Bank overdraft

Often the cheapest way to borrow money in the short term, an overdraft allows the customer to go into the red with his current account up to an agreed limit. The date by which the overdraft must be repaid is usually agreed beforehand too, but if you think that you might not be able to keep to the arrangement, you should contact the bank, in writing, asking for an extension of the facility. Interest rates on overdrafts vary with each bank's lending policy. Normally they are 3%-4% above bank base rate (currently 11%), although some banks, such as Barclays, seem to have a 'regional' policy towards overdrafts, and charge as much as 12% over base rate in some branches. It is therefore important that, if you are considering an overdraft, you contact the bank to determine the rate of interest. Work out exactly how much the loan will cost before you sign any forms.

However, there are disadvantages with overdrafts — they are payable on demand and, if for any reason you cannot keep to the agreement, the bank can 'call-in' the loan. You will almost certainly have to pay interest and bank charges for the entire quarterly banking period, irrespective of whether the overdraft was repaid at some earlier time. A bank can also 'freeze' money in other accounts, transferring it into a current account, to repay an overdraft, although this does not often happen.

You may have a 'standing' overdraft facility with the bank. Be sure to repay the full amount from time to time, so there are peaks and troughs on the account. Otherwise the bank may become nervous as to your ability to repay, and start sending letters.

Bank personal loan

These can be arranged for almost any (legal) purpose, and are organised either by filling in a form, available from the bank counter, or by making an appointment with the manager or one of his assistants.

Personal loans are usually available for amounts from between £300-£7,500 repayable over a maximum of five years (three years for cars and one year for holidays). Interest rates vary between 18%-20% Annual Percentage Rate at the moment, and are usually unsecured. Sometimes a down-payment is required from you so that the bank knows that you are willing to risk your own cash as well as theirs. The advantage of a personal loan is that repayments are fixed for the whole term of the loan, so that you will not suffer if interest rates later start to increase. You might, for example, use the loan to repay credit card and hire-purchase debts. This will have the advantage of reducing the interest you pay currently on all these separate agreements and will also mean that you have only one fixed monthly payment to the bank to think about. Sickness, accident and redundancy insurance is now a widespread optional extra. For a fairly modest sum, your loan will be repaid should you fall ill or lose your job.

Hire purchase

Once enormously popular, hire purchase has begun to give way to credit cards and budget accounts. Under a hire purchase agreement, the customer hires the goods for an agreed period and can then buy them on payment of an 'option fee' when the time is up. The option fee is usually very small, and transfers ownership of the goods to the customer.

Because the finance company actually owns the goods until the option fee has been paid, it has certain legal rights, if a customer falls into arrears. The company may repossess the goods if less than one third of the instalments have been paid and providing the company has given the customer seven days' notice of its intentions. Staff or representatives of the company are not permitted to enter the customer's property without his agreement.

If more than one third of the instalments have been paid, the company must get a court order for repossession. If the customer has tried to be reasonable, given the circumstances, the judge may not automatically award the order, but can suspend it, subject to repayments continuing and to an agreed reduction of the arrears over a 'reasonable period' of time. This means the judge will fix a set amount of arrears (usually quite low) which are to accompany the normal weekly or monthly payments until the debt is settled.

It is illegal to harrass or coerce a debtor to pay up. The current maximum penalty for doing so is a £2,000 fine.

Credit sale

With this form of agreement, the customer owns the goods from the outset, but undertakes to pay for them over an agreed period. Since the finance company has no powers to repossess it must sue for recovery of the debt, not the goods. Credit sale is a popular method of finance amongst the large retail multiples, supplying electrical goods. Interest rates tend to be high; at the time of writing 37% APR is not uncommon, so while this may be a convenient form of finance, it is by no means a cheap one.

Revolving loan (cash flow account)

This is popular, especially with banks and finance houses, and often goes under the name of 'cash-flow account'. The customer borrows a multiple of an approved monthly payment; for example, 20 times a monthly payment of £30 = £600. A cheque book might be issued on a separate account enabling you to buy whatever you choose with the money. Each month you make an agreed payment, in this case £30, of which a proportion will go towards the interest charged monthly on the account, and the remainder pays the capital balance of the amount borrowed. You can 'top-up' the loan from time to time, according to the balance in the account.

This can be a convenient way of obtaining goods whenever you choose, without having to apply for loans all the time. One big disadvantage with this type of arrangement is that interest rates are high; and if the account is run up to the maximum sum, more and more of the monthly payment goes towards interest, with the effect that the loan can take a very long time to repay — and costs a fortune in interest.

Leasing

In effect, the finance house buys the equipment, for example a television, and leases it (hires it) to the customer at an agreed rental. At the end of the period, the customer may decide either to 'lease' new goods or continue to use the original equipment at a very small rental, known as a 'peppercorn rent'.

The unique feature of leasing is that it completely separates use from ownership. The customer uses the equipment as he pleases, and in the case of a television, retains all the benefits of service and maintenance, but never becomes the owner.

There are schemes, however, known as lease-buy agreements, which enable the customer to purchase the equipment at the end of the period. Interest rates in the 'consumer' sector of leasing are usually very high.

Credit cards

These have become so popular that many high street stores prefer them to cash. There are around 1,200 different cards available in this country, and a total of 44 million of them are tucked away in wallets and purses at any one time. *Access* alone receives around 69,000 new applications a month.

Credit cards are operated by subsidiaries of the big banks and, in simple terms, enable you to buy now and pay later for a staggering array of goods and services. To obtain a card you simply complete a form available at your bank and send it to the card company. They run the usual checks to ensure that your financial record is clean, and then send you a card. This takes three to four weeks. You are given a credit limit and you can use the card in any approved store and spend anything up to your limit.

About four weeks after the very first time you use the card, you will receive a statement itemising all your transactions and where they took place. You have 25 days to clear the entire amount or any proportion in between – the minimum being £5.00 or 5%, whichever is the greater. If you clear the account within the 25 days you pay no interest, which means that you have had seven weeks interest-free credit. If, on the other hand, you choose to pay only a small amount, or the minimum payment, interest is added to your account on a daily basis (currently around 27% APR), and continues to accrue until you pay it off.

You can use the card to obtain cash advances from your bank at home or abroad and to purchase anything from fur coats to petrol. However, if you allow your spending to reach the credit limit and pay back only small amounts, you will pay very handsomely for the privilege. This is how your repayments are applied:

1. Interest from all previous statements.
2. Interest on any cash advances.
3. Capital on any cash advances.
4. Interest on purchases.
5. Capital on purchases.

Credit card companies are often criticised for raising credit limits without asking the customer. Many people feel this is some form of 'privilege' and unwittingly get themselves into deep debt. If your credit card company increases your limit without your permission, write to the Customer Services Department, asking them to refrain from doing so in the future. You can have your limit decreased again if you wish.

There is no doubt, however, that the credit card, properly used, can be a tremendous asset in personal financial planning. Take the example earlier of being able to pay for goods over a seven-week period without incurring interest. This is fine if you are able to exercise willpower in your spending, and know when to stop and send in your payments (in full). Most people use their cards as a second income which, in times of hardship, can be very dangerous. It is also extremely easy to obtain several cards without any of the companies being aware of the fact. Credit card companies do not exchange information and have no way of knowing, unless there are court judgements against you, how many other cards you may be holding. Indeed, anybody over the age of 18 would have little or no difficulty in getting around £4,000 credit from the average British high street in the space of a few hours.

In theory, it is possible to use credit cards as a permanent source of cash, calling on your bank balance only once in a while to clear the outstanding amounts. In practice, however, this requires great discipline, and is not recommended.

Store cards

These have been hailed as the most powerful marketing tools ever devised and are used by the giant retail multiples as weapons in the 'market-share' wars. It is claimed that since store cards encourage customers to be loyal to a particular store chain, they spend between two and six times more in one place than they would using old fashioned cash.

As with credit cards, you have a financial limit and can use the card(s) to buy any of the goods in the store. Some companies operate cards on a 'revolving loan' basis — the customer pays a fixed amount each month until the balance is cleared, or he wishes to buy more. If you have a nil balance on your account, your monthly payments actually become savings and start earning you interest. Other companies operate their cards on the usual credit-card principle. Either way, it is big business and profits are high. This is easily understood when interest rates are examined. Since APRs of 37% are not untypical this method of credit can be extremely expensive if allowed to get out of hand.

The cost of credit

Under the law, all instalment credit agreements must show how much the customer will have to pay for getting credit. This cost, or 'credit charge', is expressed in three ways.

1. As a cash sum. This represents the amount a customer will have to pay over and above the amount borrowed. For example, if you borrowed £900 you might have to pay it back in 24 monthly instalments of £46.50, meaning that you pay back £1,116 in all. Therefore, the credit charge would be £216.

2. As a flat rate. If the credit charged is expressed as a rate of interest on the original sum borrowed, the £216 is equivalent to an annual 'flat' rate of interest of 12% on £900 over 24 months.

3. As an effective annual percentage rate (APR). If the amount borrowed were repaid in one sum at the end, the 'flat' rate and effective annual rate would be the same. However, because the amount borrowed is gradually repaid over the period, the effective annual rate is greater, in this case, 23.8%.

Always check to ensure that any offer of credit is accompanied by the annual percentage rate, since working on the flat rate alone is very misleading. If a flat rate only is quoted, the following calculation will enable you to find out the APR.

'Flat' rate = 12%

APR = 12% x 1.984 = 23.80%

As a general rule of thumb, the APR is between 1.8 and 2 times the 'flat rate'. In this example we have used the figure of 1.984 to determine the APR of 23.80%.

Finance houses

Finance houses were arguably the pioneers of instalment credit in the UK. They were formed during the 1860s to provide funds to colliery owners who could not afford the cost of railway wagons needed to transport coal. The finance houses bought the wagons directly from the manufacturers and hired them to the colliery owners. Although, traditionally, finance houses concentrated on lending into the commercial and industrial sectors, by 1965, 65% of all lending was made to private consumers. This has fallen back to some extent, and currently finance house lending to consumers accounts for around 43% of the total, or £5bn. In 1986 nearly £2bn was advanced for the purchase of new and used cars. The most significant growth area, however, has been for home improvements and property loans.

Finance houses, via the Credit Card Group, offer a wide range of credit-card facilities and revolving credit schemes, both directly and through high street 'private label' facilities. £751m or 15% of total lending to consumers took this form in 1986.

For all practical purposes, borrowing from such an organisation is the same as borrowing from a bank. Legislative proposals currently under discussion will seek to remove the legal distinction between banks and most finance houses, and in all other respects the consumer benefits equally under the law.

How instalment credit works

In most types of instalment credit agreement, the customer makes a minimum down-payment, usually a stated percentage of the cash price of the goods. The down-payment or deposit is deducted from the cash price, and the balance is provided by the finance house, which adds its own 'credit charges'. The resulting sum is divided by the total number of instalments to find the amount of each payment. For example:

Cash price of goods	£1,350
Less: deposit 33⅓%	£ 450
Balance of cash price	£ 900
Add: Credit charges over two years based on £900 @ 12% 'flat rate' per annum	£ 216
Total sum payable:	£1,116
£1,116 ÷ 24 (months) =	£ 46.50 per month

NOTE: The Annual Percentage Rate of interest is 23.8%

Minimum deposits have varied over the years from nil to 50%, and are controlled by government decisions to expand or deflate consumer spending.

Mortgages

Millions of people apply every year to banks, building societies and finance houses for funds to buy a home of their own. It makes sense to go into debt for this purpose because most people would never be able to save up enough cash to buy a home, and the increase in property values generally far outpaces inflation and virtually all other formalised savings schemes. In certain areas of the country during 1986, however, house prices actually did fall, due to unemployment and a generally harsh economic outlook.

There are three main types of mortgage available, and these are annuity (or repayment); with-profits endowment; and low-cost endowment.

Annuity mortgage

This is where the sum advanced, usually over 25 years, is repaid in amounts of interest and capital. In the early years, most of the repayments go towards paying the interest element of the mortgage, but this gradually reduces over the term as more and more capital is repaid. At the outset of the mortgage, a mortgage protection policy is usually taken out, which is a one-off payment covering the life or lives of the mortgagors. Buildings insurance is also required, and this is usually arranged by the mortgagee (lender) on behalf of the purchaser, and at the purchaser's cost.

There are advantages of the annuity mortgage, particularly in the early years when tax relief on the interest of the mortgage can be reclaimed in full. As the interest reduces, however, so does the tax relief, and this, combined with probable pay rises over the period, begins to make the repayment method unattractive.

With-profits endowment mortgage

With this type, the buyer pays only the interest element throughout the entire term of the mortgage. A life insurance policy is taken out and monthly payments go towards the eventual cash value of the policy after 25 years, or however long the term is. The mortgage is redeemed when the proceeds of the matured insurance policy are made over to the lender; however with this type of mortgage, there will be a cash balance left over for the purchaser. The amount of these 'profits' depends on the size of the monthly insurance premium paid.

As with annuity mortgages, interest rates are subject to fluctuation, but the insurance premium remains the same for the whole term. This is a popular form of buying a home as it also incorporates an element of saving, even though the eventual profits are in the remote future.

Low-cost endowment mortgage

This method is very similar to the 'with-profits' type, but with little or no savings value in the insurance policy. The monthly premiums are therefore lower, although the interest rate will probably be the same. This method of home buying is particularly attractive to first-time buyers, for example young couples on a tight budget.

Another type of mortgage has recently been introduced in the UK, the option mortgage. This gives the purchaser the option to take out the loan at a fixed rate of interest for say, three years, after which the scheme is reviewed. The purchaser can then convert the mortgage to one of the other types or agree a new, three-year fixed-rate term in the light of the financial climate over the preceding years. The option method is very attractive at a time of low interest rates.

Second mortgage

Thousands of people qualify for second mortgages by virtue of the equity in their property (current value less purchase price). During a period of rapid and sustained price rises there is likely to be substantial equity available which the borrower can use as collateral, or security for another loan — perhaps for home impovements.

Consumer protection

The Consumer Credit Act of 1974 requires anyone providing credit or lending money under an agreement, to be licensed by the Office of Fair Trading. If a lender does not have a licence, no agreement can be enforced and the lender commits a criminal offence. It is wise to ensure that the credit organisation is licensed to deal in consumer credit before starting any negotiations. The Finance Houses Association can provide details of licensed members (it is a condition of membership that finance houses are licensed). See Appendix.

There are, however, three instances when a licence may *not* be required. They are:

1. If the agreement is over £15,000 (for example, a second mortgage).
2. If the interest rate charged is low.
3. Building societies do not need a licence.

Mortgage and credit brokers

There are restrictions on the fees which brokers can charge on agreements up to £15,000. Over this amount, a broker may charge whatever he likes, provided he obtains credit for the customer within six months — otherwise the maximum he may charge is £3.

When credit is not granted

Not everyone who applies for credit is accepted. This is because the credit reference agency may have found a record of county court judgements or other factors which would incline a lender to refuse a loan. Sometimes the information on the credit or electoral registers is incorrect or inaccurate. But the law does enable a customer to see his credit file (if one exists) at any time. If credit of below £15,000 is refused the following steps should be taken:

1. The customer must ascertain from the lender i.e. finance company, mortgage broker, retail store etc. whether they used a credit reference agency. The customer has 28 days from the time credit was refused to approach the lender, who has seven days thereafter to provide the name and address of the agency. If the lender refuses, he is committing a criminal offence which carries a maximim fine of £1,000.

2. Having acquired the name and address of the agency the customer should write, requesting a copy of his file or a letter from the agency stating that one does not exist. There is a £1 fee for this which should accompany the customer's letter of request.

3. If there are inaccuracies on file, the customer should notify the agency in writing, giving them the opportunity to put matters right. The agency must contact the customer stating whether or not it has done so.

4. If the customer is dissatisfied with any decision the agency makes he can send a correction notice of not more than 200 words, which must be placed on file.

5. If the agency refuses to do this the matter can be referred to the Director General of Fair Trading for arbitration.

6. If the Director General finds in favour of the customer, the agency can be fined up to £1,000 for each offence of refusing to comply with the customer's requests.

Chapter Nine

Bankruptcy: what it means and who is affected

Bankruptcy is a legal process by which a person who is unable to pay his debts can either petition for his own bankruptcy, or his creditors can do it to him. It is usually the culmination of a long, hard battle for financial survival. At best, under new legislation, a debtor can be allowed to continue in business, under what is called a voluntary scheme of arrangements, which is entered into by the debtor, his creditors and an insolvency practitioner (usually a specialist accountant). If all goes well, and the debtor is able to repay his debts under the scheme, he will be spared the full rigours of bankruptcy. If not, his creditors can ask the court to adjudge him bankrupt, as a result of which he is likely to lose virtually everything he owns, and more besides.

Bankruptcy can happen to anyone, though most usually to businessmen, limited liability companies and sole-traderships/partnerships. However, a new breed of bankrupt is emerging from todays 'debtor' economy — the ordinary individual, neither company director nor self-employed. Anyone with debts in excess of £750 can be bankrupted, though it is unlikely that a creditor would use this threat as a first recourse. The Insolvency Act of 1986, which came into effect on December 29, 1986, has brought about much-needed reform in some areas of bankruptcy, notably the period of time until discharge; but this has not been universally helpful. The law is so new that courts, accountants and insolvency practitioners are still feeling their way, finding out if the reforms are ultimately workable.

In simple terms, bankruptcy means that your creditors can no longer come to you for money. The Official Receiver (or, in other cases, the insolvency practitioner) legally blocks them from doing so. In return, most of your assets are 'seized' and sold to pay the creditors, and you must remain in a financial limbo for a specified period of time – two or three years for first-time bankrupts. Severe restrictions are placed upon you, which effectively stop you from leading a normal life, at least in the financial sense, although this often spills over into your personal life.

Bankruptcy is intended to wipe the slate clean, and after serving the two-or three-year term, the bankrupt is discharged and allowed to carry on as before; in other words, you have a fresh start. The intervening years, however, can be nightmarish and soul-destroying. You must try to recover assets and make 'voluntary' contributions to the creditors, often leaving you and your family at subsistence level.

The trauma of bankruptcy often triggers a series of other crises, occurring in rapid succession, which most non-bankrupts would probably not experience in the entire course of their lives. A recent survey carried out by The Association of Bankrupts in Lancaster revealed the following incidence of 'life traumas' experienced by 100 bankrupts. The figures are expressed in percentages.

Trauma	**% experienced**
Divorce	62%
Loss of home	86%
Serious illness physical/mental	36%
Loss of livelihood	92%

These traumatic events do not take into account the shocking emotional experience of bankruptcy itself, which must rate highly in the stress league. Bankruptcy then, is clearly more than a legal procedure designed to divest the debtor of his assets; it can be a life-long experience from which recovery is sometimes impossible. That is why it is so important to be aware of what even a small debt can lead to, if not properly tackled immediately. Bankruptcy should be avoided at all costs — yet strangely, there are instances where the debtor could actually benefit from the legal protection of bankruptcy; providing, that is, he is able to withstand the knock-on effect of the accompanying life traumas. For example, a recent case portrayed a family where the husband had lost his job, and although he had managed to find temporary work abroad, the contract ended and he was back on the dole. They fell in arrears with the mortgage and had other unsecured debts of around £5,000. Their building society foreclosed and the house was sold for £12,000 — £10,000 less than they paid for it. This meant that they were left with a total debt of £15,000 and no means whatever to pay. Yet the pressure being exerted by creditors was such that the family suffered acutely from the stress and worry of their circumstances. In a case as hopeless as this, the husband would probably benefit from bankruptcy, as the slate would be wiped clean after two years. In the meantime, of course, he would be subject to the normal restrictions which bankruptcy imposes. In this case, the advantages afforded by the legal protection of bankruptcy would probably outweigh the disadvantages.

During the past five years around 35,000 people have gone bankrupt, and over 100,000 companies have gone into liquidation (which is a separate legal process from bankruptcy, though often ends in the same way for those concerned). If we begin to imagine the numbers of spouses and children also involved, it is not difficult to see the huge scale of the problem.

Individual voluntary arrangements

A person having difficulty paying his debts can apply to the court for a voluntary arrangement of his affairs. The arrangement is primarily intended for those with substantial assets, where the debtor's income is derived from a beneficial use of those assets. It is unlikely, therefore, that many 'ordinary' debtors would qualify for such an arrangement. Assuming that the debtor has sufficient assets to qualify, this is how the scheme works.

Example 5: John Smith (Orrigibles) and Co.

John Smith's business has a cash-flow problem and his creditors are worried because he cannot settle his debts in the short term. John Smith knows, however, that his long-term prospects are good. To protect himself and his business, he can apply to the court for an individual voluntary arrangement. To do this he must show his current financial situation by completing an extremely lengthy and complex document, known as his proposal. He must show all his assets and whether they are secured or charged to any creditors, and all his liabilities. He must also explain why he wishes to enter into such an arrangement, and why it is in his creditors' best interests.

Although the bankruptcy rules do not stipulate that he should seek advice from an insolvency practitioner who is capable of understanding the complexity of the documents and able to set up the scheme properly, it is a sensible approach. (Look in the telephone directory under Official Receivers). At the same time as applying to the court, he must also notify his creditors of the application, and inform the Official Receiver. The court will fix a day for a hearing and, in the meantime, can block or stay any actions for debt brought against John Smith, regardless of how far advanced they may be.

At the hearing the insolvency practitioner, known as the nominee, will be asked to prepare a report on the debtor's financial affairs in time for the next hearing, usually between 14 and 28 days hence. John Smith is obliged to assist the nominee in any way required, so that the report can be brought properly before the court. It is in his own interests to do so, otherwise the court may dismiss his application. There are sanctions if he refuses to co-operate — after all, it is his proposal!

At the next hearing the court will consider the full proposal and decide whether to put it to the creditors, or dismiss it. If it is dismissed, John Smith's creditors will probably bankrupt him immediately. In this case, however, the proposal is put forward for consideration. The nominee arranges a meeting of creditors, who may either attend personally or by proxy. A chairman is appointed who puts the proposal to the creditors. If necessary, the meeting can be adjourned for 14 days to enable further information to be brought forward or for creditors to seek instruction from fellow board members or legal advisers. Ultimately, the meeting must decide whether to accept or throw out the proposal. Once again, if it is thrown out, John Smith will be bankrupted. However if 75% of the creditors, by value of their claims, accept his proposal, he will be allowed to stay in business. In other words John Smith may have 10 creditors, but if only two of them account for 75% of his debts, and agree to 'keep him alive' the others would have to go along with them, according to the Bankruptcy Rules.

The chairman of the meeting then compiles a further report to the court, detailing the outcome of the meeting and any resolutions passed — for example, should one nominee replace another. The person brought in to oversee the plan is called the supervisor of the scheme. Immediately that happens, John Smith must hand over all his assets to the supervisor, who now has complete control of his affairs. If John conceals any assets or refuses to co-operate, the supervisor can petition for John's bankruptcy. The arrangement continues for as long as it takes to pay all the creditors and costs of the court, nominee and supervisor. In total, these can be very heavy.

In summary, an individual voluntary arrangement relies upon the goodwill of creditors and the co-operation of the debtor to allow his assets to be worked in a controlled way in order to pay off his debts. The scheme is likely to apply only where there are substantial assets available.

Creditor's petition

If Jim Jones owes £750 to one creditor, or a total of £750 to a number of creditors who decide to band together, technically, he can be bankrupted. The creditor must serve on Jim Jones a Statutory Demand.

Details of the document

This is a complex and bewildering document for anyone who is not an accountant or solicitor. It contains details of the claim which the debtor must either admit or defend within 21 days. In practice, he has only 18 days in which to prepare his affairs if he disputes the demand. The Statutory Demand must satisfy certain provisions if it is to be upheld. These are:

1. The amount of the debt (or aggregate amount) must be equal to or exceed £750.
2. The debt must be for a fixed sum, and not for damages as yet undetermined. The debt must be payable either immediately or at some certain future time, and must be unsecured.
3. The debtor must appear to be unable to pay or to have no reasonable prospect of being able to pay the debt or debts.
4. There must be no outstanding application to set aside a statutory demand served in respect of the debt or any of the debts.

Statutory demands

Under the Insolvency Act of 1914, a creditor could petition for a debtors' bankruptcy only after satisfying certain conditions with the court. It was the court which issued the petition to the debtor. Now the creditor can issue a statutory demand without any reference to the court. In other words, the debtor is effectively assumed guilty until proved innocent at a subsequent hearing.

The new law provides for a debtor to be able to prove or establish to the satisfaction of the creditor(s), that a debt payable at some certain future time will be paid. In other words, Jim Jones borrows £2,500 over three years from a loan company to buy a car. The loan is unsecured. Jim falls ill and writes to the company explaining that he may be unable to pay for a while. The company can issue a statutory demand which, if not dealt with to the company's satisfaction, can entitle Jim's creditor to commence bankruptcy proceedings on the basis of the future debt.

There is certain information which must be provided on the statutory demand. It is:

1. The purpose of the demand and the fact that if the debtor does not comply with it, bankruptcy proceedings may be commenced against him.

2. The time within which the demand must be complied (usually 21 days) in order to avoid bankruptcy proceedings.
3. The methods of compliance which are open to the debtor.
4. The debtor's right to apply to the court to set aside the demand.
5. The demand must specify one or more individuals whom the debtor may contact in order to secure or compound the debt — that is, reach an agreement on how it is to be paid to the satisfaction of the creditor.

The court knows nothing about the statutory demand until either the debtor applies to have it set aside or the creditor petitions for bankruptcy. If the debtor applies to have the demand set aside, he must do so within 18 days. This is mentioned only once on the form, in small print.

The demand must be served personally except where the creditor has made a number of attempts to effect personal service without success. He may then leave it with the debtor's secretary or assistant, so long as he can show that the debtor would have seen the demand on a certain date.

In some cases the statutory demand can be served by running an advertisement or series, in one or more newspapers. If the debtor has solicitors acting for him, the demand could be served on them and they in turn must bring it to the debtor's attention.

Setting aside the demand

There are only four grounds upon which a statutory demand can be set aside. They are:

1. The debtor appears to have a counter-claim, set-off or cross-claim equal to, or in excess of, the amounts specified in the statutory demand; this means that if the debtor has some property which could be secured to the creditors in settlement of the debt, or, if he is in business and can show that the creditor owes him money equal to or more than the amount of the claim, the statutory demand could be set aside.
2. The debt is disputed on grounds which appear to the court to be substantial.
3. It appears that the debtor holds some security in respect of the debt claimed by the demand.
4. The court is satisfied on other grounds that the demand ought to be set aside.

In categories **1** and **3**, the position is quite clear. If a creditor has served the demand knowing that the debtor has a counter-claim or some security by which the debt could be settled, he has acted very unwisely, and the statutory demand will be dismissed.

The remaining grounds, **2** and **4**, are the cause of some concern from the debtor's point of view. In **2**, the debt is disputed on grounds which appear to the court to be substantial. This literally means that the debtor, without any prior proceedings or knowledge of the court, can be brought to the verge of bankruptcy on the face value of the statutory demand served by the creditor. In all other areas of civil law, the defendant has only to establish a *prima facie* or arguable defence, but here he must have substantial grounds for the demand to be set side. The burden of proof lies solely with the debtor to prove his innocence, not with the creditor to prove the demand.

In **4**, the court is satisfied on other grounds that the demand ought to be set aside. This probably refers to the way in which the demand was served, whether the facts and figures are correct, and so on. It does not refer to the merits of the case or whether there is a defence.

Bankruptcy

Bankruptcy petition

If the court dismisses an application to set aside the statutory demand, it can order the creditor to present a bankruptcy petition immediately, or on a date specified by the court.

The petition is filed at the court along with an affidavit, verifying the petition. A deposit of £112 for the official receiver has to be paid by the creditor. The petition is then endorsed by the court with a date and place for the bankruptcy hearing, and a copy is sent to the debtor, or served personally.

Bankruptcy hearing

It is vital that the debtor attends the hearing. It could be the most important day of his life. The debtor, either personally or through his representatives will have the opportunity of having the bankruptcy petition dismissed if the court can be satisfied that he is able to pay all his debts, or that, having made an offer to the creditor(s) to secure or compound the debts, it has been unreasonably refused.

Example 6:
Jim Jones, who borrowed £2,500 from a loan company, has worked out that if he were made bankrupt and all his property were sold, there would be £500 left over after all the secured creditors had been paid. Jim offers this to the loan company, who refuse it on the ground

that it is unreasonable. It seems likely that the court might rule in Jim's favour as the economics of the situation show that Jim's offer is reasonable in the circumstances.

But if Jim Jones cannot satisfy the court that he is able to pay his debts, or that there is no reasonable prospect of him doing so given his income and liabilities, the court will adjudge him bankrupt.

Small bankruptcies level – (applicable only on debtor's petition)

If the debtor's estate on bankruptcy is £20,000 or less, and providing he has not been bankrupt within the previous five years or entered into any arrangements with creditors, the court may order the summary administration of the bankrupt's estate. This means that he will have a much easier time of bankruptcy and will be discharged, subject to certain conditions, in two years. In other cases, the usual time until discharge is three years.

Debtor's petition

This is where the debtor asks the court to make him bankrupt, possibly to protect himself and his family from pressures from creditors, or if he knows that his situation is hopeless and that it is only a matter of time before a creditor serves a statutory demand. It may seem strange, but it costs money to declare oneself bankrupt. The debtor can apply to a county court, and on payment of a £112 deposit, must complete a statement of affairs, detailing assets, liabilities, and the general financial background and circumstances which brought him to this position.

The court then fixes a date and time for a hearing, and may, if it thinks fit, dismiss the debtor's own application if there is a possibility of coming to a voluntary arrangement with creditors. In this event, the court will appoint an insolvency practitioner to prepare a report (as in the individual voluntary arrangement earlier) which will then determine whether this is feasible. If not, the court will uphold the petition, and the debtor will be bankrupted for a period of two or three years, according to the circumstances.

Bankruptcy order

A bankruptcy order by the court begins as soon as the debtor is adjudged bankrupt, and from that moment onwards, all personal property, with the exception of clothing, bedding, essential tools of the debtor's trade and basic domestic requirements, are vested in the official receiver or trustee in bankruptcy. His property becomes part of his estate, which is administered by the official receiver or trustee, until he is discharged. It is their job to sell off the assets of the bankrupt for the benefit of his creditors, and to manage the debtor's affairs throughout the term of bankruptcy.

Who are you dealing with?

The examiner or inspector

After the bankruptcy hearing, the debtor must pay a visit to the Department of Official Receivers to compile his statement of affairs and to be 'examined' by a member of the receiver's staff on his conduct and dealings prior to the bankruptcy.

Although the debtor is supposed to complete the statement of affairs, such is the length and complexity of the document, that the examiner, more often than not, does it for him.

During the first meeting (there may be several), the debtor must take with him all financial documents relating to his property, insurances, bank account, cheque books, credit cards and so on. If he owns a car, he must hand over the keys too. The examiner then asks a number of prescribed questions which are designed to piece together the jig-saw puzzle, and draw conclusions as to how the debtor came to be in this mess. It is an offence to conceal information from the examiner which, if discovered, could lead to contempt of court. The examiner is not there to pass judgement or heap scorn on the debtor; in fact, he tries to be as helpful and sympathetic as circumstances allow, so long as the debtor 'comes clean'.

The inspector

Normally within seven days of the bankruptcy order, an inspector is sent to the debtor's home to make an inventory of his assets. Anything not belonging to him will be disregarded, but the owner may have to swear an affidavit, claiming ownership. If the debtor tries to hide, sell or otherwise dispose of his property in order to confound the inspector, he commits an offence which carries severe penalties. Anything belonging to his spouse or children will not be included in the inventory.

The agent or auctioneer

When the inspector has finished with the debtor, a copy of his inventory is normally sent to an agent or firm of auctioneers for valuation. The debtor will not be told what value has been placed on his goods. Any third party who is unconnected with the bankruptcy can make an offer to buy back some or all of the goods involved. This may sound expensive but depending on the condition and value (new) of the goods, they can be bought very cheaply indeed.

The reason for the low return on these goods is as follows. The costs involved in removal and storage are very high. Your goods may lie for months or years before they are sold, and even then it is unlikely that many people would be interested in buying everyday, 'run of the mill' furniture and effects from an auction, unless of course, they were valuable. If the debtor can find someone to back him, then he may soon have all of his property back again (in point of fact, it is rarely moved from the bankrupt's home until absolutely necessary). He will not own the goods though, but can use them 'on loan' from whoever bought them. If someone is going to buy your goods back, they should contact the official receiver for the name and address of the agent or auctioneer. The first offer should be low, no more than one quarter of the value of the goods, and probably less. The offer can always be revised if it is refused.

The official receiver

The receiver is a very powerful figure. He is a civil servant attached to the Department of Trade and Industry, and is also an official of the court, and has wide ranging powers available to him. He may summon a meeting of the creditors, or be asked to convene one, if 25% (by value) of them agree. In cases where the bankruptcy is the subject of a Certificate of Summary Administration, he may act as trustee of the bankrupt's estate.

The receiver can, at any time during the bankruptcy, apply to the court for a public hearing at which the debtor's affairs will be aired before the court. Under the old law, a public hearing was mandatory, unless the official receiver requested a dispensation order. The notice of a bankruptcy is advertised in *The London Gazette* and a local newspaper.

The trustee

The trustee in bankruptcy, like the official receiver, is very powerful. He is appointed (or removed) either by the court, the official receiver or after a meeting of the creditor's committee has been held.

His function is to seize and dispose of the assets of the bankrupt's estate in accordance with the Insolvency Act. He is entitled, subject to certain provisions, to use his own discretion in managing the estate as he sees fit.

The trustee can take any property a bankrupt acquires after the bankruptcy order was made, providing he does so within 21 days of the acquisition and notifies the court. He can also take away tools of the bankrupt's trade, books and so on, if he thinks that they could be sold for a higher price than the cost of a 'reasonable replacement'. To do this, he must apply to the bankrupt and the court within 42 days of the bankruptcy order.

The trustee has extremely broad powers over the affairs of the bankrupt, and, in some cases, has been known to have been unremittingly harsh in the execution of his duties.

Income payments order

This is an important new aspect of the law and one which could have very severe consequences for the bankrupt and his family. If the bankrupt is earning, the trustee can apply to the court, claiming payments for a specified period, and even up to discharge. The terms on which a payments order can be made by the court are crucial, as can be seen from the wording in the bankruptcy rules: 'The Court shall not make an Income Payment Order, the effect of which would be to reduce the income of the bankrupt below what appears to the Court to be necessary for meeting the reasonable domestic needs of the bankrupt and his family'.

There is no published guidance as to what is meant by 'reasonable'. However, it is felt that this may mean that bankrupts and their families will have to survive on levels of income equivalent to supplementary benefit, if the trustee applies for the balance of earnings. (Note: At the time of writing, the full rules concerning the Insolvency Act 1986 have not yet been published.)

Who gets what

Unsecured creditors, in the main, are very unwilling to bankrupt anyone because they know that the chances of them getting anything are extremely remote. Here are the details of who gets what and the pecking order of creditors.

Fully secured creditors

The bank, building society or finance company who own your home (if you are paying a mortgage) are fully secured. If you have a second mortgage this, too, is also fully secured on your property. Your house, or whatever else is the security, will be sold to repay the fully secured creditors first. Although the rules demand that your property must be sold at a 'fair market price', it will go up for sale at auction where it will not fetch its real market value. It is sold at auction, not at a fixed price, to protect the official receiver or trustee from any comeback by the creditors, claiming that your property was 'undersold' and that their dividend was thus reduced. If the property is sold for more than the amount of outstanding mortgage, the balance passes to the receiver to be distributed amongst the partially secured, preferential and unsecured creditors.

Partially secured creditors

Imagine that you have an antique worth £500 and that you need to borrow £1,000. You borrow the £1,000 in return for giving your antique as security. Your creditor is confident that it will increase in value so that he could recover his £1,000 in the event of your bankruptcy. Now that you are bankrupt, your antique is taken and sold at auction for, say, £750. Your creditor gets the £750 and then lodges a claim as an unsecured creditor for £250. However, if the antique was sold for £1,250 your creditor would get his £1,000 and the extra £250 would go to the trustee for re-distribution amongst the other creditors.

Preferential creditors

These are normally government departments. They get paid after your secured creditors. First in line is the trustee, followed by the official receiver, the Inland Revenue (taxman), Customs and Excise (VAT) and, if you are in business, National Insurance contributions. Whatever is left over from the sale of your assets, after the secured creditors have been paid, goes to these departments. Very often there is nothing left for the unsecured creditors.

Unsecured creditors

These are companies, and possibly individuals, to whom you owe money and who do not have any security against the loans. They are at the bottom of the pile and, more often than not, must be content with 'writing the debt off' their books. Credit card companies, in-store credit, gas, electricity and telephone are all examples of unsecured creditors. That is why it is important to transfer the utility account into the name of your spouse or partner. However, you must first ensure that these accounts are settled before bankruptcy occurs, and that the spouse or partner is unconnected with the bankruptcy.

Chapter Ten

Where there's life . . .

'Bankruptcy', somebody once said, 'is like using a sledgehammer to crack a nut'. The official machine is supposed to act solely on behalf of the creditors, realising the assets of the bankrupt's estate. Nearly always, the bankrupt and his family are left bewildered and shattered by what has taken place; at the very time when support and encouragement is required they instead find doors slamming in their faces. In the UK we have a peculiarly harsh attitude to bankruptcy or 'failure', as it is sometimes known. The law regards bankrupts almost as 'non-people', such are the restrictions placed upon them, and society is encouraged to treat them with suspicion. The fact is, however, that most bankrupts are hard-working, decent, honest people, who would welcome the opportunity of paying their debts in full. Businessmen do not always become bankrupt because they are inefficient, but because market trends undermine their years of hard work.

The importance of talking

The most frequent response from the 'newly bankrupt' is to behave as though nothing has happened. This is a psychological defence against acknowledging the severity of the situation and, in time, usually gives way to a more sober appreciation of what bankruptcy involves. Some liken it to the shock of losing a loved one, others as an engulfing 'nothing', or emptiness. And since this is usually the first time that this will have happened to a bankrupt, it can only help to discuss the psychological and practical problems with friends and relatives. The more open you are about the problem the less likely you are to suffer feelings of guilt and shame at the very time when you need to be strong, not crippled by emotional side-effects. And beware the law; it tinges bankruptcy with criminality by the very sanctions it imposes, and the length of time a bankrupt must endure his punishment. In America, the system is quite different. After approximately three months the bankrupt is given a pat on the back and encouraged on his way. In many cases, American venture capitalists prefer to see one or two failures in someone's 'portfolio' before committing to a loan. That way they know that the client has first-hand experience of the potential and actual pitfalls of business.

Whatever a bankrupt feels, he must be prepared to spend the next few years in a state of financial 'suspended animation', probably living in rented accommodation and with very few of the former 'luxuries' of life.

The bankrupt and the home

Under the old law, the courts had fairly wide discretionary powers to enable the bankrupt and his family to remain in their home for quite long periods of time sometimes years. This gave the family a chance to recover from the trauma of bankruptcy, and also, importantly, to enable a spouse to raise sufficient funds to buy out the partners' stake in the home, and so prevent it from being repossessed by mortgagees or the official receiver, who would sell it on the request of the creditors.

Today, however, the situation is somewhat different. The law now clearly states that after one year has elapsed, 'the interests of the creditors outweigh all other considerations'. This means that, where a bankrupt either solely or jointly owned the home, he can expect to lose it after 12 months. The spouse, notionally, has a 50% interest in the property and, providing she is unconnected with the bankruptcy, should press the official receiver, trustee or supervisor very hard to get a fair share when the property is sold. In this circumstance, do seek legal advice.

The trustee, who is under obligation to gain a fair market price for the home (and all other assets), will sometimes allow the bankrupt to put it up for sale on the 'open market'. Otherwise, it will be sold at auction, where prices are almost always lower.

As soon as bankruptcy seems imminent, you should get in touch with the housing department at your local authority and register on the waiting list. Also, notify the Homeless Persons Unit, which will probably be able to offer some form of accommodation. Write to SHAC (see Appendix) for a list of housing associations which may be able to help too.

Gas, electricity, telephone

These will normally be cut off and restored only on changing the name of the account holder, and on payment of high reconnection charges. To avoid all this, change the name before the bankruptcy.

Bank accounts

Once bankrupted, you cannot have a bank account without the permission of the official receiver and the bank. Even then, you will be allowed only a basic 'chequing account', with no overdraft facilities or banker's card. If the account shows a credit which the receiver thinks is more than you need to live on, he is entitled to withdraw the funds from the account for disbursement amongst creditors. All in all, it is better, and safer, to deal exclusively in cash.

Prior to bankruptcy, arrange for your spouse to open a new account elsewhere, in her name, so that she will not be affected by your problem.

Insurance policies

Before bankruptcy proceedings commence, and if the policy has any savings element, transfer it solely to your spouse's name. However, be careful about the timing of this. The court may subsequently regard this action as an attempt to conceal assets from the receiver. Take legal advice beforehand. If the insurance policy is for life cover only, for the benefit of spouse or family, this will be unaffected by your bankruptcy.

Wills

An undischarged bankrupt cannot benefit from a legacy (unless it exceeds the amount of money owed). The proceeds will be seized and passed to the official receiver for disbursement amongst the creditors, after deducting costs of administrating the bankruptcy, which are usually very high.

Make sure that anybody intending to leave you anything in their will while you remain undischarged, changes it in favour of your spouse, children or trusted third party.

Pension funds

If you have invested in a pension fund to provide for your future retirement, bankruptcy will not affect your right to benefit from this. Be warned, however, that if you are still undischarged when the fund matures, the trustee in bankruptcy has the right to seize part of your income to pay creditors!

Restrictions of bankruptcy

Obtaining credit

An undischarged bankrupt can obtain a maximum of £50 credit without disclosing the fact that he is undischarged. Getting credit for more than this amount would, understandably, be very difficult once the bankrupt has 'confessed'. If it is granted, the fact should be stated in writing so that no misunderstanding can occur in the future, and also to protect the bankrupt from committing an offence, which carries a heavy penalty.

Bank accounts

See page 121.

Earnings

A bankrupt is required to make voluntary contributions of anything he earns over and above the living expenses for himself and his family. Failure to do so is an offence, and may impede the bankrupt from being discharged on time and could result in the trustee applying for an income payments order (see page 115). People living on supplementary benefit would probably not be required to pay anything at all during the bankruptcy.

Travel

Since bankrupts should not be able to afford to travel, this is a rare problem. However, if for some reason you do intend travelling you should notify the court. Permission will not be unreasonably withheld, unless there is some doubt about the bankrupt's proposed date of return or the purpose of the trip.

Business

A bankrupt may not, without leave of court, be a director or manager actively engaged in the setting up and running of a limited company. However, he may set up as a sole-trader or partnership, providing proper books of account are maintained. It is important to seek professional advice before embarking on any new venture.

Assets

A bankrupt may have any assets, which he personally acquires during the term of bankruptcy, seized and sold off. You must, however, disclose these assets. So, a person unconnected with the bankruptcy will have to act for the bankrupt, and buy everything in his own name.

Public life

A bankrupt cannot be an MP, JP, councillor or other public figure during the term of the bankruptcy, and for five years afterwards. If this really presents a problem, the bankrupt can apply to the court for a Certificate of Misfortune, which means that a person wishing to take up or resume a public career can get special dispensation from the court. In practice, this is rarely awarded.

When it's over

Obtaining a discharge

If the bankruptcy was ordered on the debtor's petition, and is the subject of summary administration (i.e. small bankruptcy, under £20,000) discharge will be automatic after two years. In all other cases (except criminal bankruptcy) the statutory period is three years from the date of the bankruptcy order. If the bankrupt has been bankrupt up to 15 years beforehand, he must then apply to the court for his discharge, which would probably be conditional upon his paying some further contribution towards his estate.

The cost of bankruptcy

The official receiver or trustee is paid according to a scale of charges, which vary with the amount of assets realised and sold off. They get a percentage on both occasions, and the table opposite gives an idea of just how expensive bankruptcy can be.

Annullment

A bankruptcy can be annulled if the bankrupt manages to pay off all his debts, plus trustees costs during the term. In reality, there are extremely long odds on this being possible, unless a windfall from the football pools or someone's will came about.

And finally . . .

It is hoped that this section on bankruptcy has put you off the idea altogether. It is one of the worst things which can happen to anybody accompanied by a crippling loss of freedom and status.

Appendix

Useful names and addresses

National Association of Citizen's Advice Bureaux
115/123 Pentonville Road,
London N1 9LZ.
Tel: 01 823 2181

National Consumer Council
18 Queen Anne's Gate,
London SW1 9AA.
Tel: 01 222 9501

Building Societies Association
3 Saville Row,
London W1X 1AF.
Tel: 01 437 0655

Finance Houses Association
18 Upper Grosvenor Street,
London W1X 9PB.
Tel: 01 491 2783

SHAC (The London Housing Aid Centre)
189a Old Brompton Road,
London SW5 OAR.
Tel: 01 373 7276

Child Poverty Action Group
1 Macklin Street,
London WC2B 5NH.
Tel: 01 405 5942

Association of Bankrupts
4 Johnson Close,
Abraham Heights,
Lancaster, LA1 5EU.
Tel: 0254 64305

Age Concern
Bernard Sunley House,
60 Pitcairn Road,
Mitcham,
Surrey.
Tel: 01 640 5431

Alcoholics Anonymous
11 Redcliffe Gardens,
London SW10.
Tel: 01 352 9779

National Marriage Guidance Council
76a New Cavendish Steet,
London W1.
Tel: 01 580 1087

Gingerbread
35 Wellington Street,
London WC2.
Tel: 01 240 0953

Shelter
157 Waterloo Road,
London SE1.
Tel: 01 633 9377

Samaritans
(see local telephone directory).

Books

How to Split Up – and Survive Financially by Tony Hetherington, Unwin Paperbacks, 1986.

The Penguin Guide to Supplementary Benefits by Tony Lynes, Penguin, 1985.

Index